COLLECTIBLE
ALUMINUM

By

Everett Grist

COLLECTOR BOOKS
A Division of Schroeder Publishing Co., Inc.

Book Design by Joyce Cherry
Cover Design by Beth Summers

COLLECTOR BOOKS
P.O. Box 3009
Paducah, Kentucky 42002-3009
www.collectorbooks.com

Copyright© 1994 by Everett Grist

The current values in this book should be used only as a guide. They are not intended to set prices, which vary from one section of the country to another. Auction prices as well as dealer prices vary greatly and are affected by condition as well as demand. Neither the authors nor the publisher assumes responsibility for any losses that might be incurred as a result of consulting this guide.

Searching For A Publisher?

We are always looking for people knowledgeable within their fields. If you feel that there is a real need for a book on your collectible subject and have a large comprehensive collection, contact Collector Books.

CONTENTS

THANK YOU

A special thanks to Jimmy Grist of Savannah, Georgia, for the loan of the purse to photograph. My appreciation to Ron and Tammy Zelnick of Longwood, Florida, for several of the better pieces as well as valuable help with the book and price guide. I also want to make special recognition of Chad Wheeler, the artist who reproduced by free-hand the hallmarks used in the book.

PREFACE

As you will notice, these photos are arranged by item rather than by manufacturer or company. This reasoning is two-fold. First, we may not readily identify a company by a hallmark which is not complete or which does not actually identify the maker by name. Second, this book is set up mainly for quick reference of pieces. When you buy a piece, you know whether it's a basket, a bowl, or a tray. So the book is set up in sections of baskets, bowls, and trays. You can turn to that section and locate your item with a complete description.

I haven't ignored companies. There is a section on companies or producers as we know them, thus far. We have so much to learn about this fascinating collectible, I can't describe to you my excitement of doing more research and cataloging of items.

My sincere hope is that this book fills a need for collectors across the country, not only to identify their aluminum ware, but to place a realistic value on it when taking into consideration the maker, the rarity, and the current demand.

INTRODUCTION

I've been chasing aluminum items for years and have about 6,000 pieces in my collection. I kept thinking that one day its time would come, but I was not sure if I would live to see it. Well, it did, and I have. Why have I spent that much time and money on these items? Just look at the photos in this book. Look closely at how an item is formed, and think about the hands-on workmanship that was inherent in producing the item. The twisted, curled, and formed aluminum rods which form the bases of candelabra were fashioned by hand. Aluminum cannot be welded. Handles, finials, and bases had to be applied with aluminum rivets by hand. (Rivets made of copper or brass are machine applied.)

The next time you look at a piece of aluminum in a box at a yard sale, or see a bowl being used as a container for a handful of collectible buttons, take a good hard *close* look. Examine the detail in the pattern. Notice how the rivets securely fasten the finial or handles. Look at the craftsmanship. If you can appreciate what I have just described, then you'll probably do as I did when I first noticed aluminum — dump out the buttons and buy the bowl!

Almost monthly, I can see an increase of prices on aluminum items in shops, at flea markets, and even at yard sales. While some of the little items such as coasters and the plentiful items such as round trays still have a fairly reasonable asking price, sellers of the larger pieces do not always realize what they possess and are under-valuing their items, which is even better for those of us already collecting. Other sellers, feeling the big boom has already hit, have their items way overpriced; I have seen many common coasters (single coasters!) priced at $6.00 and $8.00. Now, more than ever I am realizing that the market value of anything is what a buyer is willing to spend, because $8.00 coasters are being bought and sold, and yet they are so plentiful that they are found at almost every flea market and shop. I cannot see how they can command that price, but obviously someone, ignorant of their plenitude, is willing to part with the cash.

The problem facing the collector today is that aluminum is a coming collectible, and few realize which pieces are in limited supply or which patterns seem more difficult to locate, making them a rarity. That is the purpose of this book. By the values we place on the items in this book, we are hoping to give you some idea about what items are plentiful and which are the more difficult to locate. Granted, locality has a great deal to do with availability. California, with its great influx of veterans and their families after World War II, the age of "more is better", has made that area a great place to find aluminum. The mid-West has a good supply also, but not the same types of pieces. California is noted for carrying everything outdoors to cook and serving meals on the patio. Trays, relish trays, bread and roll trays, celery dishes, pitchers, and glasses were all carried out to the patio to serve guests. In the mid-West there was more of a potluck mentality. Casseroles are big in the mid-West, and many can be found with the original Fire King or Pyrex insert. Pie plate carriers and cake carriers are very plentiful. For those of us who do not travel, there are trade papers which enable us to buy, sell, and trade with collectors in other parts of the country to obtain desired items at a more realistic price than we may find in our own area.

As far as I know, there is only one book on the shelf today which goes into depth about aluminum, and very few others give it much space at all. I'll be the first to admit that we haven't even scratched the surface with what went on in that industry. We are still attempting to learn about the foundries, let alone the individual craftsmen who produced the items. There are some truly notable ones which came to the surface very quickly, but there may be others. The bane of any collector of any sort of item is the paper sticker. They are too quickly lost, and the item is then very difficult to identify. This is not unique to aluminum. I have seen Roseville pottery items which you could identify for certain only because, while the item could be located in a company catalogue, the outline of the uniquely shaped paper label was still visible on the bottom, adding credence to that photographic evidence. I have seen Rodney Kent items that had no hallmark but merely a hang-tag on the handle identifying it as an Original Rodney Kent Creation.

As with any collectible, we are always seeking new and varied information. Somewhere in the United States there are children of aluminum craftsmen, who may have kept their original pattern drawings at home or maintained possession when they retired. Somewhere are craftsmen who still have tales to tell about how the products evolved and how the companies flourished. Somewhere are persons who have one-of-a-kind prototypes. If you are one of those persons, and would be willing to share your information with the world, contact me. After all, if there is a book, shouldn't we consider a sequel with new and updated material?

Cleaning

As far as cleaning aluminum is concerned, nothing works better than soap and elbow grease. I have found that one or two trips through the dishwasher with normal dish washing powder does not seem to hurt the aluminum. However, pieces that we use and wash practically daily in the dishwasher have been left with a white corrosion from chemicals in the dish washing detergent and/or water. I have carefully cleaned badly stained pieces with soap pads. I also have discovered that following dishwasher or hand cleaning with a silver polish (the type you wipe on, let dry, then wipe off) gives the aluminum a mellow look and protects the surface for a longer period of time. Aluminum should always be thoroughly dried after cleansing.

IN THE BEGINNING

What do an 1850s Napoleonic-era baby's rattle and the cap atop the Washington Monument in Washington, D.C. have in common? Both are made of aluminum. There is no record of how much the rattle cost, but the 100 ounce ornament which serves as a lightning rod cost $225,000.00 in 1884, a time when many families lived on less than $2.00 a week. Aluminum was known from ancient Egypt and Persia where aluminum silicates were used for pottery and "alums" were used for vegetable dyes and medicines. Prehistoric people fashioned weapons, jewelry, tools, and religious icons from iron, bronze, and copper, but metallic aluminum, aluminum without "contaminates," remained unknown. In 1782 Frenchman Antoine Lavoisier postulated the existence of pure aluminum as "the oxide of a metal whose affinity for oxygen is so strong that it cannot be overcome either by carbon or any other known reducing agent."[1]

During the time that the earth was cooling down from the spate of volcanic action that formed the continents, aluminum dissipated, combining with a multitude of other substances. This made it difficult to isolate, and difficult to merely identify. Among other things, aluminum forms the basis for many precious and semi-precious stones. Bonded with oxygen it forms blue sapphires and red rubies. In a more elaborate concoction it forms the myriad greens of jade. Jewelers and artisans at the time of King Tutankhamun, as well as contemporary Navaho and Zuni fashioned jewelry from a substance called turquoise ranging in color from blue to green, which is nothing more than a little aluminum dust mixed with phosphate. Isolate aluminum and you have a light, strong material that can be infinitely molded, poured, pressed, or hammered into shape, but therein lays the problem—isolation of the aluminum.

Technologically, aluminum in one of the most difficult to separate from other elements which surround it. It cannot be "panned" in the manner gold and platinum are gleaned from streambeds around the world. It cannot simply be smelted or refined out as one would iron or copper. Rather an additional process is needed to break down the adhesion of the aluminum to its companion elements or contaminates.

While aluminum was first hypothesized as a possible element in 1782, it was not positively isolated and identified until 1807. An Englishman, Sir Humprey Davy, accomplished this feat, a ho-hum discovery at best. Interest in the metal was *extremely* limited. From a negative aspect, a handful of scientists thought it only as a novelty with which to dabble. From a positive aspect, the Court of France became obsessed with this new metal which shone with a luster like silver. The tables of nineteenth century France were adorned with handcrafted serving pieces and eating utensils consisting mainly of knives and spoons. Forks were a latecomer insofar as flatware is concerned, because people were still basically eating with the utensils God gave them—their fingers.

Aluminum became a fashion statement of the time. It was a suitable substitute for and more fashionable than either gold or silver. Why would this overly abundant metal be considered fashionable? Simply because it was more expensive. Only the rich could possess it, and, thus, it became more desirable among the elite.[2]

Aluminum has always been aesthetically pleasing with its silvery color and high luster. It is light but strong, and probably most important, it is resistant to corrosion. Unlike iron, it does not rust. It does not corrode as copper, nor will it tarnish like brass. It was envisioned by Napoleon III as having great military potential as light armor, but it remained exorbitant in price. Napoleon could have more cheaply clad his soldiers in gold.

From the time of Davy's discovery in 1807 to the mid-1850s, many chemists, inventors, and scientists experimented with aluminum and methods of refinement, some with a modicum of success. However, between 1854 and 1859, another Frenchman, Henri Sainte-Claire Deville, truly refined the production of metallic aluminum. Where aluminum had been priced at $550.00 in 1853, it dropped to an unbelievable $17.00 per pound in 1859![3]

It was not until early 1886 that an inexpensive sodium reduction method of smelting aluminum became known. Charles M. Hall, working in a makeshift laboratory in his Oberlin, Ohio, kitchen made the discovery and the cost of aluminum was reduced to $4.00 a pound.[4] Hall applied for the patent five months later and established a then legal monopoly. As sole owner of the patent, he had the power to sue anyone who attempted to copy his method, giving him free reign to transform his metallurgical process into a lucrative commercial venture. That patent, U.S. No. 400,766, became the principal asset of The Pittsburgh Reduction Company, the corporate predecessor of Alcoa.[5]

A salesman as well as an inventor, Hall persuaded six friends and family members to advance $20,000 to support the trial development of his new process. On October 1, 1888, The Pittsburgh Reduction Company was formed and the investors were to learn that Hall really knew what his discovery was all about! By the mid-1890s The Pittsburgh Reduction Company was operating the largest smelting complex in the United States at Niagara Falls, New York, and a fabricating plant in New Kensington, Pennsylvania, making aluminum ingots and aluminum sheets or blanks for an emerging national market.[6] Also by that time, Pittsburgh Reduction was smelting aluminum by electrolysis, an even more economical method than sodium reduction. In 1895 the firm sold some 920,000 pounds of aluminum for about $0.54 a pound.[7]

Within the early corporate history of today's Alcoa, it seems that the only thing that went amiss was the name. Although chartered as The Pittsburgh Reduction Company, a "reduction" firm or one that "reduced" a commodity, was normally thought to be one that reduced animal carcasses to commercial products such as hides and tallow. Therefore, prospective customers might look at Pittsburgh as a company that dealt in piglets rather than ingots. Another misconception was outlined by Edwin S. Fickes, the company's chief engineer, who said, "(The name)…The Pittsburgh Reduction Company…did not indicate the business in which the company was engaged [by 1907]; moreover, the name of the company was often confused in Pittsburgh with the name of the American Reducing Company, a local concern engaged in garbage collection and disposal, to the great annoyance of telephone operators and mail clerks."[8]

True to the nature of corporate America in the early days of the twentieth century, the company was renamed Aluminum Company of America: big, bold, factual—transitory. By the late 1920s the name "Alcoa" was registered as a trademark for ingots produced at the New Kensington plant. Within 10 years the press, the courts, and the company itself often used "Alcoa" as a shortened version of the legal corporate name.[9] (By that time, Aluminum Company of America was embroiled in court hearings regarding the monopoly which had been established by Charles Hall 30 years before.)

Where does all this increased production and reduced cost lead us? Simply here. From the time of the $0.54 a pound aluminum of 1895 until 1910, the fastest-growing application of aluminum was cookware. In fact, up until a time just before World War II, the public's primary exposure to aluminum in any form was through items found in their kitchens. Sure the metal was used in commercial applications, and some of it was found in airplanes and automobiles, but how many ordinary citizens of 1939 availed themselves of air travel and how many owned automobiles? A very small percentage.

Ever the salesman, Charles Hall had his sales staff out beating the bushes for customers to buy his aluminum ingots. By 1899 Pittsburgh Reduction Company was trying to convince manufacturers of cast iron teakettles, pots, and skillets to use aluminum to cast teakettles, but they weren't buying. So back to square one! They had a product with no takers.

Pittsburgh Reduction had to create a desire for their product. They approached cooking utensil manufacturers more softly than the manner in which they had attempted to browbeat the cast iron manufacturers, expounding on the natural attributes of the metal. Aluminum was shiny, lightweight, highly conductive, and acid-resistant. Why, it would save money, because it could cut down on the amount of fuel used to cook food. Aluminum was that heat-conductive! It was easily kept clean, had a pleasing appearance, and had no harmful effect on food products.[10]

However, the soft-sell method did not work either. To overcome this problem, Arthur Vining Davis "borrowed" a molder from the Griswold Company in Erie, Pennsylvania. The name Griswold was then and is today known as one of the prime producers of cast iron cookware. Eli Griswold had a lion's share of the American cookware market. If only they could convince Griswold to use aluminum… Griswold's molder was brought to New Kensington to cast an aluminum teakettle. It was something that would make Eli sit up and take notice, something that would show Griswold why he should buy Pittsburgh Reduction's aluminum ingots and make his utensils out of this beautifully bright, shiny metal. Was Davis successful? Yes and no. He failed, because he did not convince Griswold to buy aluminum ingots. He succeeded, because Griswold ordered 2,000 teakettles from Pittsburgh Reduction. This offer to buy confronted Pittsburgh into a "Hobson's Choice" situation. They could either add a fabricating unit to their New Kensington works specifically for the production of cast aluminum utensils or lose the order. They chose to expand their production.[11]

While Pittsburgh Reduction continued to produce the rolled aluminum sheets which were much more desirable, because the manufacturer only had to stamp out the utensils, it still created problems. First, Pittsburgh Reduction was not the only producer of sheet aluminum, and many products on the market were thin and inferior in quality to Pittsburgh's own. When inferior products hit the market, aluminum cookware got a bad rap, and while Pittsburgh made a more superior product, it suffered along with the producers of the inferior aluminum. Second, the ultimate consumer did not know how to care for aluminum, and the manufacturers were faced with mass customer dissatisfaction. Yes, aluminum does discolor, and it can pit, blister, or scale; but these are signs of poor maintenance, not of a poor product, and it was solvable.

This two-fold problem was eventually solved with one swoop. First, in 1901 Hill, Whitney & Wood, a company which purchased sheet aluminum from Pittsburgh Reduction and stamped out cookware, went bankrupt while owing Pittsburgh a good deal of money. Unable to collect what was owed them, Pittsburgh Reduction made a deal to take over the manufacturing equipment and assets of Hill, Whitney & Wood with the goal of continuing the production of stamped cookware, while striving for the high quality they wished to maintain.

Now, any company will tell you that their customer list is among their most prized assets, and Pittsburgh Reduction noted that John Wilson and Charles Ziegler were among Hill, Whitney & Wood's most lucrative. It was also noted that they had an unfilled order for 2,800 kettles from Wilson. Wilson and Ziegler were contacted, and Pittsburgh Reduction was well on its way to solving its second problem of how to teach the customer the method for maintaining aluminum cookware but in a rather circumventive maneuver.

Ziegler had put himself through medical school by selling enamelled kettles door-to-door. Wilson had been a house-to-house book canvasser in his college days. In 1895 they joined forces to sell Handy Kettle Steamers and The Ideal Percolating Coffee Pot. They purchased the items in a partially-fabricated state, finished the assembly, and sold them directly to the consumer.[12]

First, we see Pittsburgh Reduction with a method of maintaining quality, i.e., they make their own items via the Hill, Whitney & Wood connection. Second, they have a means to instruct the ultimate consumer on how to maintain their cookware, because they will sell directly to the consumer and instructions will be part of the sale. Incidently, what Zeigler and Hill were teaching the customer was that sodium hydroxide, a substance used in making some soaps, quickly attacks aluminum ware. While the ware was not affected by ordinary water, alkaline, or soapy water could cause discoloration of the metal. Aluminum had to be dried; if water was allowed to dry on it or sit in it for long periods of time, elements in the water caked on the aluminum which could cause pitting and blistering.[13]

So as not to drop the ball here, Pittsburgh Reduction organized a wholly-owned subsidiary, known as the Aluminum Cooking Utensil Company, which was operated by Wilson and Ziegler, and the rest is history. If Aluminum Cooking Utensil Company doesn't sound familiar, does the name WearEver ring a bell? As I said, the rest was history.[14]

After 1907 when Pittsburgh Reduction became Aluminum Company of America, the firm expanded, ultimately producing cookware at New Kensington, Arnold, and Logan's Ferry, Pennsylvania. Between 1935 and 1939 the average annual sales of all types of cookware nationwide was 63,900,000 units. Aluminum alone accounted for 33,200,000 units, or 52% of the market; this despite a myth being circulated that aluminum poisoned the foods cooked in it.[15]

Needless to say, by the time Alcoa cornered the market, charges of unfair monopoly and the alleged cut-throat treatment of competitors had the company in court. The break of Alcoa's hold on the aluminum market opened it up for a myriad of smaller companies to begin the production of aluminum cookware. It also opened up the market for small forges and creative entrepreneurs to fashion the lovely accent and serving pieces which are quickly becoming sought in today's secondary market.

It cannot be discounted that decorative as well as functional aluminum pieces were the rage from the 1930s through the 1950s, and there is a revival of items from Art Nouveau to the fabulous fifties which add to their collectiblity today. They were the rage due primarily to the aesthetic appeal and the reasonable cost. While the rich could indulge their sense of beauty with silver plate if not sterling silver, those on more modest means relied on the gleam of aluminum to spark up their table settings and interior decor. Is this not reason enough to collect the items today?

Aluminum lent itself to objets d'art and furniture alike during the Art Deco period. It lent itself to the "more is better" decorating styles of the 1950s when returning G.I.s and their families finally set up housekeeping. This was the romanticized time when Dad worked days at his old job, went to school nights on the G.I. Bill to better himself, and bought a little house on a G.I. Loan, while Mom stayed home to decorate their little two-bedroom bungalow to look just like those in the magazines. If this sounds simplified or if you doubt our generalization of the times, pick up a *Ladies' Home Journal* or other women's magazine from the 1950s and see if you don't get that feeling from the advertisements, the recipes, and the articles. Of course, this is not meant to cast aspersion on that period in time. Were it not for those of us who wish to hold on just a little bit to those simpler times, there would be no collectors of items from that period. Baby-boomers, cars with fins, sonic booms, and round screen televisions are all very nostalgic and romantic. There are a whole host of items out there to seek, and a bountiful choice in patterns on those items. You could collect for years and not get one sample of each item in each pattern. Doesn't that sound delicious, to be able to collect for years and not get a duplicate?

A comprehensive list of the manufacturers, both large and small, of wrought, hammered, or spun aluminum pieces will be years in the compilation. We know a good many of them: Alcoa-Kensington, Rodney Kent Silver Co., Canterbury Arts, Cromwell, Crown Aluminum, Everlast, World Hand Forged, Wrought Faberware, Federal Silver Co., Continental Silver Co., Wendell August Forge, DePonceau Aluminum Craft, Arthur Armour, Buehner-Wanner, and Farber & Shelvin, just to name a few. As you will notice, producers of silver pieces also jumped on the bandwagon, not wishing to miss out on that middle-income range of consumers. All found aluminum to be a wonderful medium in which to display their talents.

While most makers used 100% aluminum, some producers chose a 98.5% aluminum/1.5% magnesium alloy. Whichever was chosen, the material was ductile, meaning it could be worked cold. It could be drawn, pressed, spun, stamped, and hammered into form without heating.

Many finishes could be produced to add beauty and style to a plain tray or dish. They were frosted, scratch brushed, polished, burnished, sand-blasted, painted, grained, colored, and anodized. Highly-polished items which sparkled in the candle light, were available. If your thing was chrysanthemums, you could get a myriad of serving pieces in that pattern treated to stand out against the hammered background. The consumer was limited only by her own vision of what decorations she wished in her home.

The finishes named above are defined as follows:[16]

Dipped or Frosted: the piece is dipped in an alkalai or acid solution which "eats" into the normal sheen of the aluminum, leaving it with a matte finish. This is a surface suitable for painting.

Scratch Brushed: the surface of the piece is scratched with a fine steel or brass brush which leaves a satiny sheen; it diffuses light with a pleasing effect.

Polished: a four-step process. The piece is first rubbed with a fine powder on a cloth buffer. Next it is rubbed with oil, then buffed with powder again. Finally, the piece is buffed with a colored powder to bring out the characteristic bluish-white of the aluminum.

Burnished: in contrast to a frosted finish, a stone, wood, or steel tool is used with a lubricant against the item to give a high luster.

Sand Blasted: gives a white frosted finish; also employed as a preliminary step to scratch brushing, dipping, or painting.

Painted: to paint, the piece must be frosted, dipped, scratch brushed, sand blasted, or scoured with emery paper. (Never use lead-based paint.)

Grained: after polishing, the piece is held against a soft pine wheel revolved at high speed on a lathe.

Colored: Black brazing can be done by painting with alkaline or neutral solution of cobalt nitrate following by heating. The color varies from steel gray to black. Or paint with solution of 60 gms. copper chloride in 300 cc of water to which ammonia has been added.

Anodized: Subjecting a metal to electrolyte action as the anode of a cell in order to coat with a protective or decorating film.

So, you have items from which to choose and patterns on those items. There are companies and finishes from which to choose. You can mix and match your collection, or you can specialize. Best of all, you can utilize your collection. With concern for the finish, you can use your aluminum items daily without having to worry about depreciating their value as a collectible. So, collect, use, and enjoy your aluminum.

COMPANIES

Many companies produced aluminum items, and we may never have an entire list. While most manufacturers stamped their items with hallmarks, many of them used only paper stickers. Also, on some pieces the lid goes on a glass bottom, both of which may or may not then sit on top of an aluminum tray. If there is a tray, it is usually the only marked piece of the three. The glass dish usually had a paper sticker, and the lid was unmarked. The first time you wash one of these items, the sticker comes off. When we're dealing with just a lid and a glass dish, it is difficult to determine who made the piece.

As you collect, you will learn the patterns and how to distinguish manufacturers. Once a pattern is identified, you will be able to correlate it to unmarked pieces. You'll make mistakes at first, but the more you study, the more distinctive patterns will become.

Some companies were merely trade names for the large department stores. We all recognize the Kenmore brand as being a Sears product, but how many of us remember that Harmony House was also a Sears trade name? There were big companies and small companies; companies that produced a multitude of items, and companies that specialized in fewer designs. There are the old companies, the new companies, and the imports. And let's not disparage the imports, because Nasco has a few nice items on the market. Some of the pieces marked Japan are a little shoddy, but nice ones have also been seen. We are probably looking at immediate post-war items and then items made into the 1960s and 1970s. Some of them are even newer. Many collectors feel the light weight, plain, nondescript pieces most likely date from the 1960s. Importers began flooding the marked with Japanese items, attempting to compete with the Italian and Spanish manufacturers who were producing items of higher quality. But "Japan" does not equate to "shoddy." There are nice pieces from Japan; there are shoddy pieces from Japan. The same can be said for Italy. And let's admit it, the same can be said for the U. S. of A.

Herein is a list of companies and hallmarks. It is not nearly complete, nor is it self explanatory. We know that Arthur Armour had at least three hallmarks and Wendell August Forge at least seven. Buenilum, a trademark of the Buehner-Wanner Company, had a minimum of three hallmarks, and Continental had three. Even "Hand Forged" is seen in two designs, and we're not sure if this was a company name or just a statement of the production method.

Hallmarks were added to the piece after it was finished, along with any product number, etc. The hallmark was made up onto a stamp or die. The die was positioned on the bottom or back of the aluminum piece and hammered to force an indentation of the die into the aluminum. These dies occasionally wore out or pieces broke, creating the need for a new one to be produced. Since the dies were made by hand, they were not always identical from one model to the next. This is what caused the wide variety of designs on hallmarks, even within one company.

The same can be said for the design itself. These designs were not created as leather designs are, with each little detail being stamped with a separate tool. They are on a plate, much like a printer's plate. The plate is positioned on the blank, and a machine pushes the design into the aluminum. Now, I was really disappointed when I discovered this, because I thought they sat down like leather toolers do and got that design going all around by free-hand. The work is basically done on a little scribing plate. The scribing plate works for so long (like the hallmark die), and then they have to be recut. That's where you get the different designs on pieces. Whoever recuts the design does not always follow it exactly. The stems might be longer and the leaves in a little different position, but they still call it the same pattern. If bowls suddenly become a half inch wider and an inch shorter, the design will not fit and has to be recut to fit the blank. That is why we must study, study, study, to see the basic similarities in patterns.

We now know that Alcoa was the mother of all aluminum, because it held the monopoly on aluminum for so many years. While Alcoa did not directly produce the profusely decorated, highly-sought pieces we collect today, they did have a direct impact on their production.

Wendell August Forge

Wendell August was a blacksmith, and generally, we think of blacksmiths as shoers of horses and repairers of horse-drawn farm equipment. The truth is that many blacksmiths were artisans at heart. When aluminum became available, Wendell August used its adaptability to decorative uses to enter the business of architectural enhancement. He was commissioned to create the entrance gates at Alcoa's New Kensington, Pennsylvania, plant and subsequently was commissioned to created hammered aluminum trays for company executives. Founded in 1923, this forge is still in operation and is the only forge producing items totally by hand. Since all work is totally hand produced, it is up to the artist to approve the piece for sale. That is to say, it was declared a quality piece before the hallmark was stamped.

Wendell August sold his business in 1984. After that time, whoever was working in the foundry designated specific markings as their signature. They were allowed to put those markings, called touchmarks or artists' marks, beside the hallmark of the Wendell August Forge. Each design was assigned to a specific artist, and took the form of a cloverleaf, diamond, triangle, star, etc. One looks like a flame. We might add that after August sold the business in 1984, a lot of people in Spring City, Grove City, and the surrounding area started little smithies producing aluminum.

The earliest products from the forge are very, very thin, having little weight at all. They were also hallmarked differently. Some of the really early productions merely have WENDELL in straight block letters stamped on them. We also find "Patent Applied For" stamped either straight or in a curved line.

Arthur Armour

Although no longer producing, Arthur Armour had great impact on the production of aluminum wares. A graduate of Carnegie Tech with a degree in architecture, Armour designed patterns for the Wendell August Forge. A self-taught forger, he went into competition in 1934 and produced many of the highly sought items on today's market.

Buenilum

Highly polished pieces with precise beading around the lip and other edges such as bases, and heavy-gauge aluminum seem to have been a must for Buehner-Wanner Company, and their pieces are substantive. They, too, had a gimmick with finials and posts, theirs being a ball with a cone attached. Aluminum rod handles were twisted and looped and sometimes both. Fairly simple in design, the beading and the finials gave an elegant look to the otherwise plain Buenilum pieces.

Canterbury Arts

Rivaling Rossi for artisanship were two Canterbury Arts designers: C. C. Pflanz and J. Hattrick. However, their signatures are not found on the backs of the pieces as Bruce Fox's signature is. On the very arty pieces the artist's signature will be hidden in the design itself. These pieces generally have a silvery look.

Canterbury Arts was also one of the leaders in the production of intaglio pieces. The opposite of repoussé, intaglio designs sink into the metal, and some collectors mistakenly call it etched.

Continental Silver

Continental started out as a silver company and many of the silver patterns were reproduced in aluminum. Early American Style are Continental products.

This company is probably most noted for its chrysanthemum pattern. Extremely well executed, this pattern is found on almost all pieces offered, both large and small. Together with the chrysanthemum, Continental added a leaf at each end of the handle, and if the piece is handleless, then two leaves were placed opposite each other on the rim or lip of the piece. The leaves were incorporated into a base for a chrysanthemum bud finial and as the thumb rests on candleholders.

Cromwell Hand Wrought Aluminum

Nothing is known, thus far, about Cromwell, other than their pieces were highly decorated and well-made. For the most part, they used aluminum rods, twisted and shaped, for handles. Many pieces had a very precise honey-comb hammered background or all-over pattern. All pieces are of highest quality.

Crown Aluminum

You don't see much Crown Aluminum, and if you do, it's the anodized stuff. For the most part, collectors don't keep track of the anodized aluminum, only the signed pieces. Beauty Line also produced anodized pieces.

DeMarsh Hand-Forged

DeMarsh evidently worked within the Wendell August Forge in Pennsylvania and moved to Florida in the 1960s, setting up his own forge in St. Augustine. He closed the forge in St. Augustine and moved to Deland, Florida, and he's still there today. So, you have DeMarsh Forge; DeMarsh Forge, St. Augustine, Fla.; and DeMarsh Forge, Deland, Florida on the hallmarks. Anything marked St. Augustine is before the mid-1970s. It has been reported that the forge is still there, but DeMarsh no longer works it as a business. He has produced special order items in recent years and enjoys it as a hobby today.

DuPont

DuPont of Chautauqua, New York, is a relative unknown. The items are very reminiscent of the better-day Wendell August or Arthur Armour. We really don't know whether DuPont worked for either one of them, but a lot of the patterns are similar. It is as if he worked for them then started off on his own.

Everlast

Everlast seems to have been one of the most prolific manufacturers of collectible aluminum. The company also incorporated both intaglio and repousse methods into their production. Known to have at least eight different hallmarks (with the polar bear found only on coolers or ice buckets), Everlast produced a wide variety of items while keeping their quality at a premium. One of their prettiest and most desirable patterns was Bali Bamboo, wherein the bamboo shape was incorporated even into the handle. Trays, relish trays, and other servers for moist foods contained compartmented glass inserts. These are more often found today than the aluminum counterpart, indicative of the change of taste when the first popularity of aluminum lost its sheen.

Everlast also made meat servers, and they can be found with meat-trees on the bottom which drain the drippings away from the meat itself. The biggest problem with these items is that they score very easily, so it's difficult to find one in really good condition.

Neocraft is an Everlast product, and many items are marked Neocraft by Everlast. Lehman Aluminum Hand Forged is actually an early Everlast, too.

Farber & Shlevin and Farberware

Mention Farber & Shlevin, and most collectors will identify with pattern inserts in trays. F&S used Indian Tree, Colonial Dancers, Victorian scenes, and Greek urn china inserts on many trays and servers, but there was also a candy dish or basket with a bowl. Many pieces are marked on the china, i.e., Limoges, made for Farber & Shlevin, while the aluminum contains no hallmark whatsoever.

Farberware produced "frames" for china from Shenandoah Ware and glass from Cambridge Glass. To me, one of Farberware's most notable patterns is the Stem of Berries. It is well done, well embossed, and just nice to see. This company was also known for its flower stem and finial in which the stamen of the flower twined about the stem. A hallmark on top of the piece, so to speak.

Forman Family

This company produced some intriguing pieces, although their use of a light-gauge aluminum turns off some collectors. They, too, had a chrysanthemum pattern, but it is not nearly as striking as Continental's. They produced covers for New Martinsville glass dishes to make butter dishes and candy dishes. Open flower finials and open-work floral handles are often seen.

Kensington

Kensington of New Kensington was Alcoa's contribution to this collectible. The company has a very strong following for their unique creations. These are spun aluminum items rather than hammered, and while it does not appeal to all, it allows for the wide variety of tastes.

Kensington produced items for cocktail parties and buffet service, i.e., a more sophisticated clientele than the backyard and potluck entertainers. Use of brass handles and ornaments added a definite touch of class to the clean crisp lines. As with other companies, Kensington produced an alloy using aluminum as the base. The product was a metal which retained its high polish while resisting fingerprinting and scuffing. It also does not pit as does most aluminum ware.

Rodney Kent

Rodney Kent probably one of the most recognized artists just by examining a piece. Rodney Kent Silver Company produced a tulip pattern which is very distinctive, but even more so is his use of flower and ribbon motif handles. Handles on casseroles have the ends of the ribbons tied in bows, and the flowing ends of the ribbon form the feet of the piece. Pieces with lids have tulip flower finials with flower ribbons around the base of the finial. Kent pieces were all darkened for contrast, so the designs literally jump off the piece at you. They are ornate; they are well executed; they are beautiful. It is no wonder that they are so popular with collectors today.

There is some Rodney Kent out there that is very thin and is unmarked. Sad to say, they are Rodney Kent items made toward the end of the company's existence.

Keystone Ware

This company most likely had a parent company whose identity has yet to be discovered. Keystone seems to have entered the aluminum production field late in the popularity period and exited early. One of their most distinctive patterns was the all-over vine and flower design trays. It is really quite striking. Some handle designs copied Buenilum without the finial. There is a great following for this company.

Regal Ware

Regal did not produce many pieces, but what they did produce was well made. Pitchers are plentiful, and I have heard of a set of glasses which matched the pitchers. The only other pieces we have run across so far are tiny, almost miniature, salad servers. They are very well made, but so tiny that it could be considered miniature instead of collectible aluminum.

Natale Rossi

Natale Rossi is another Wendell August Forge break-away. August trained out-standing designers and producers of aluminum with Arthur Armour and Natale Rossi being probably two of the best. (A third one, probably less known, went west and produced Made in California By TOWN items.)

Rossi is credited with the discovery of the repoussé technique of decoration. Repoussé had been used for years in jewelry, being merely the raising of a design by hammering on the backside of the material being worked. While repoussé work can be cumbersome and not totally appealing, Rossi's work is of the finest workmanship and his are the most intricate designs.

The producers listed above seem to have produced the bulk of the more sought pieces. That is *not* to say that these are the only collectible producers. Bruce Fox and Palmer-Smith made lovely pieces that are highly collectible. (It is Fox, not Cox. Sometimes you find a paper label with a red fox pictured with his name on it, too. You really have to use your imagination to see Fox rather than Cox on his signature.)

Bascal (Italy) is one of the few desirable anodized aluminum products. Usually it is not marked "Made in Italy." It is very popular, and it is going very strong in the anodized market. However, it may hurt the market as the new pieces are out-pricing the old anodized pieces.

Pieces with non-company hallmarks such as Hand Finished, Hand Forged, Hand Wrought, etc., are lovely pieces that add to any collection. However, so little is known about these companies/producers there is no need to use space here to tell you that we have few hard facts. But we will keep researching and add information to future books.

A list of companies and hallmarks we have collected to date are listed on the following pages. Are these all of them? Probably not. Will we ever know all of them? Probably not. Isn't it exciting? A collectible that we can research and study and collect...maybe for a lifetime...and not know it all or have it all. There are hundreds of areas in which we can specialize if we wish, or we can attempt to have it all.

Admiration Products Co., *see* 38A, 38B

Aluminum by Laben *see* 41

Arthur Armour, *see* 1-A, 1-B, 1-C

Avon, *see* 51

Baricinni

Bascal (Italy), *see* 47

Beauty Line

Best

Bruce Fox, Wrought Metals, Inc., *see* 48A, 48B

Buehner-Wanner (produced Buenilum pieces) *see* 3A, 3B, 3C

Burger of Miami, *see*, 40

Carrib, Miami, Fla.

California Made (Wrought by L. Whitney)

Canterbury Arts, *see* 4A, 4B

Cellini Craft, Inc. (also marked Argental)

Chase

Clayton Seasley

Club Aluminum

Color Craft, *see* 55

Continental Silver Co., *see* 5A, 5B, 5C

Coronet

Cromwell, *see* 6 ?

Crown Forged Aluminum, see 7A

Delft by Crest Silver, see 25

DeMarsh Forge, *see* 42A, 42B, 42C

DePonceau Aluminum Craft, *see* 45A, 45B, 45C

Designed Aluminum, *see* 8A 8B

Early American Style, *see* 26

Embossed Aluminum, *see* 35

EMPC (an Everlast logo),

Everbrite (Italy), *see* 52

Everlast Forged Aluminum, *see* 9A, 9B, 9C, 9D, 9E, 9F, 9G

Farber & Shlevin, *see* 10A

Farberware, *see* 11

Federal Florette Design, *see* 27

Federal Silver Co., *see* 12A, 12B, 12C

Floral, *see* 56 ?

Forman Family, *see* 28A, 28B

Fry

Gailstyn (Aluminum by Gailstyn), *see* 13

Griswold

H. Mansfeld

Hammercraft, *see* 14A, 14B

Hand Finished Aluminum, *see* 29

Hand Forged, *see* 15A, 15B

Handarbeid

Handwrought Aluminum, *see* 33

Harmony House (a Sears trade name)

Hawthorn, *see* 31

Henry Miller

Hull of Meriden, *see* 23

John W. Finley - Hand Wrought

Kensington of New Kensington, *see* 30

Keystone Ware, *see* 17A 17B, 17c, 17D

Kraftware, *see* 18

Kromex, *see* 43A, 43B

LA Hand Forged, *see* 58

Laird Argental, *see* 59

Langbein Handwrought, *see* 60

Leroy Deloss Forge

Lehman Aluminum Hand Forged, *see* 37

Leumas Handcrafted Giftware

Mansfield-Handcraft-P.P.P. Co., *see* 53

McClelland Barclay, *see* 39, 39B

Millcraft Hand Wrought

Mirro

Modern Handmade

NA (Cinn. O.), *see* 50

N.C. JL Td AT (The Aluminum Works, Stratford-on-Avon England)   Also shown as Sona Ware

N.S. Co., *see* 61

Nasco Italy, *see* 44A, 44B

Natale Rossi

National Silver Co., *see* 19, 20

Neocraft by Everlast, *see* 36A, 36B

Palmer Smith, *see* 21

Perco, *see* 64

Regal Ware, see 32

Revere

Rodney Kent, *see* 16A, 16B,

Royal Hand Wrought, *see* 57

Royalty Aluminum, *see* 62

Roycraft

Russel Wright

Sona Ware

Stanley

Stede

Stratford on Avon

Sunburst (Italy), *see* 46A, 46B

Sunlite Aluminum

Town (marked Hand Made Aluminum By Town Made in California), see 63

Viko the Popular Aluminum

Warrented Aluminum, *see* 34

Wendell August Forge, *see* 2A, 2B, 2C, 2D, 2E, 2F, 2G

Westbend, *see* 49

Wilson Specialties, *see* 24A, 24B

World Hand Forged, *see* 22A, 22B

Wrought Aluminum

Zephyr Ware, *see* 54

HALLMARKS

All hallmarks shown are in our collection although some pieces are not shown due to photographing problems. Aluminum is hard to photograph, because some highly polished pieces reflect light intensely, making the pattern hard to see. Other items have dulled and are also reluctant to share their pattern in normal photography.

ARTHUR - ARMOUR

1A

1B

1C

2A

2C

HAND MADE FOR

TRIANGLE SPRINGS

DUBOIS, PA.

2D

2B

HAND MADE

2E

2F

WENDELL AUGUST FORGE
PAT. APL'D FOR

2G

21

BUENILUM
HANDWROUGHT

3A

BUENILUM
MADE IN U.S.A.

3B

BUENILUM
MADE IN U.S.A.

3C

4A

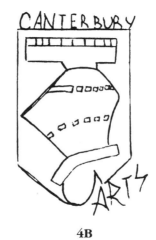

4B

5A

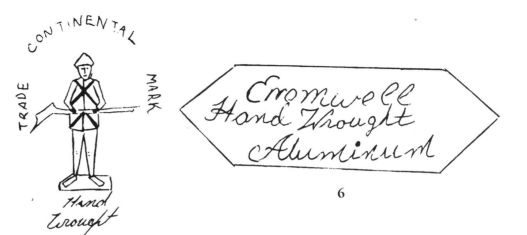

5B

5C

6

Crown Aluminum

7

8A

8B

9A

9B

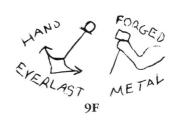

9C

Everlast
HAND
FORGED

9D

9E

9F

9G

10A

11

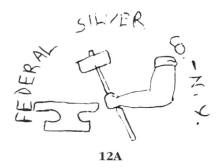

12A

ALUMINUM BY
FEDERAL
Silver Co.

12B

HANDWROUGHT
BY
FEDERAL S. CO.

12C

ALUMINUM
BY
GAILSTYN

13

HAMMERCRAF,
HAND
HAMMERED

14A

HAMMERCRAF
HAND
HAMMERED

14B

HAND FORGED

15A

HAND FORGED

15B

16A

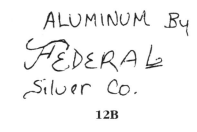

Hand Wrought
Creations
by
Rodney Kent

16B

KESTONE WARE

53

R

PAISLEY
ALUMINUM

17A

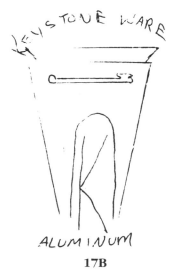

KEYSTONE WARE

53

R

ALUMINUM

17B

17C

HAND HAMMER
PATENT
PENDING

17D

18

NATIONAL SILVER

19

N.S. CO.
HAND HAMMERED

20

PALMER-SMITH

21

22A

WORLD
HAND FORGED

22B

23

24A

24B

25

EARLY AMERICAN STYLE

26

FEDERAL FLORETTE DESIGN

27

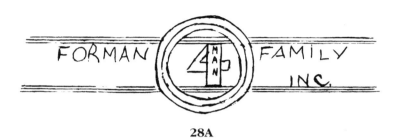

FORMAN FAMILY INC.

28A

FORMAN 4 WARE

28B

HAND Finished Aluminum

29

IK

Kinsington

30

Hawthorn ®

MADE IN U.S.A.

31

Regal suprem QUALITY Aluminum Regal ware

32

HANDWROUGHT ALUMINUM

33

WARRENTED ALUMINUM

34

EMBOSSED ALUMINUM

35

Neocraft

36

Neocraft EVERLAST METAL

36B

37

ADMIRATION
PRODUCTS CO.
NEW YORK N.Y.

38A

ADMIRATION
PRODUCT CO.
WROUGHT ALUMINUM
NEW YORK NY.

38B

(M)Celland Barclay

39A

SKY TOP

(M)Clelland Barclay©
Hand Made

LODGE

39B

40

41

42A

42B

42C

43A

43B

Nasco
ITALY

44A

NASCO - ITALY

44B

DE PONCEAU

45A

DE PONCEAU
CHAUTAGUA. N.Y.
100%
HAND MADE

45B

DE PONCEAU
GROUE CITY PA.
100%
HAND MADE

45C

Sunburst

46A

G.R.
Sunburst
MADE IN ITALY

46B

Bascal
MADE IN ITALY
G. R.

47

Bruce Fox

48A

BRUCE FOX WROUGHT METALS INC.
NEW AIBONY, IND

48B

SERV-IT

Roaster Broiler Server

A PRODUCT OF
WEST BEND Aluminum
West Bend Wis U.SA.
Item No, 311?
PATENT NUMBERS
2,270,061
DES, 146,519
Other PATENTS
PENDING

49

PAT. PEND ⟨N·A⟩ CINN.O.

50

PAT 266918
N. C. J.
STRATFORD ON AVON

51

EVERBRITE
ITALY

52

H MANSFELD
PENNSYLVANIA

53

LIGHT METALS CORP
Zephyr ware
LOUISVILLE K.Y.

54

Color Craft

55

FLORETTE
DESIGN

56

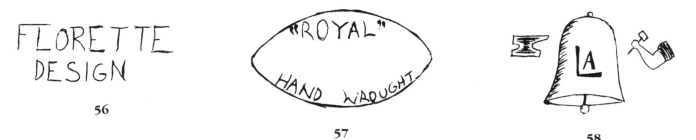

57

58

59

LANGBEIN
HANDWROUGHT

60

61

62

HAND MADE
ALUMINUM
MADE IN BY
CALIFORNIA TOWN

63

64

PICTORIAL PRICE GUIDE

Architectural piece. A screen door guard, consisting of two wrought panels with three x-braces in each. The center panel is a heron standing in water. 21" wide x 55" tall. There is no hallmark or manufacturer's identification of any type. **$225.00**

Ashtray. Left is engraved AUGUSTA NATIONAL GOLF CLUB above the golfer and THE LITTLE MASTERS, APRIL 15, 16, 17, 1966, below. 6" square. Right has the familiar duck scene, but it is more ornate and larger than most. The center is about the same size as a coaster, but the overall diameter is about 6". Hallmark: 2B (Wendell August). Left, **$35.00**; Right, No Mark. **$10.00**

Ashtray. Pine cone pattern. 6" diameter. Hallmark: 2A (Wendell August). **$75.00**

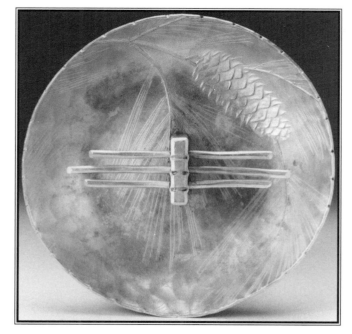

Ashtray. Left has a single holder. Bamboo pattern. 5" diameter x ¾ deep. Hallmark: 9C (Everlast). Right is a three holder ashtray in the daisy pattern. 6" diameter. Hallmark: 9B (Everlast). Left, **$15.00**; Right, **$20.00**

Ashtray set. A nice decorative piece which is also functional. The six petals of the large flower are removable, becoming small individual ashtrays. Petals can also can be turned around and fit into the holder to create an open flower. 9" long x 6" tall in the present configuration. Hallmark: 50 (N.A., Cincinnati, OH). Set **$35.00**

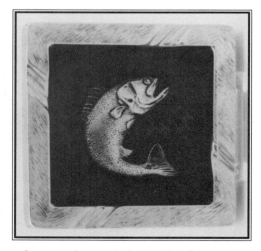

Ashtray. It has a nicely detailed fish, probably a bass, in a jumping position. A really nice piece because of the detail and the nice large size. 6" square. Hallmark : 48A (Bruce Fox). **$50.00**

Ashtray. A three holder with the head of a hunting dog superimposed over a shotgun with two flying ducks in the background. A nice hammered piece. 6" diameter. Hallmark: 9 F (Everlast). **$35.00**

Ashtray. Left is square with two water lilies and pads, sometimes called a lotus pattern. 6" square. Hallmark: 1 A (Arthur-Armour). Right is a round three holder ashtray with a leaping marlin figure. 4½" diameter. Unmarked. Right, **$35.00**; Left, **$25.00**

Ashtray. Square with a sailboat on the water. 4½" square. Hallmark: 2A (Wendell August Forge). **$25.00**

Ashtray and smoking stand. Pine-cone pattern on base, tray, ash-bowl and cigarette holder. Twisted wrought pole. 22" tall. Hallmark: 2A (Wendell August Forge). **$375.00**

Basket. Tomato pattern around edge of tray which has a serrated lip. Double handle meets in a square knot. 11" diameter x 6" tall. Hallmark: 9B (Everlast). **$10.00**

Basket. Square basket in the chrysanthemum pattern. Strap type handle has "finger waves" at top for ease of handling with applied leaves on either side. 8" square x 6" tall. Hallmark: 5C (Continental Silver). **$35.00**

Basket. Chrysanthemum pattern. Bowl comes up sharply then flares more shallowly to the 8" diameter. Single square handle has twisted hand-hold in center at top. 5" tall. Hallmark: 28 (Forman Family). **$10.00**

Basket. Sailing ship. 9" diameter. Hallmark: 12A (Federal Silver Co.). **$40.00**

Basket. Nice round basket in chrysanthemum pattern. Nicely decorated edge on bowl. Strap handle edged in same pattern as bowl applied to tab cut out of rim which allows handle to fold down. 9" diameter x 7" tall. Hallmark: 15 (Hand Forged). **$10.00**

Basket. Floral pattern in bottom with hammered rim. Serrated edge. Single round hammered handle with two inside loops. 10" long x 8" wide x 7" tall. Marked: Japan. **$5.00**

Basket. Flowering plant and wheat spray design. Fluted bowl with serrated edge. Single strap handle has finger waves at top. 9" diameter x 4" tall. Hallmark: 15 (Hand Forged). **$5.00**

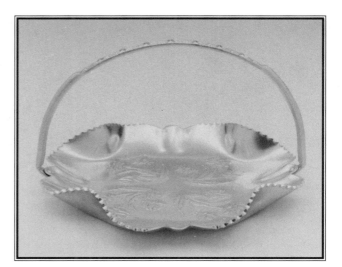

Basket. Poinsettia design in fluted basket with large serrations on edge. Single round handle is decorated in a spiral. 7" diameter x 5" tall. Hallmark: 10 (Farber & Shlevin). **$5.00**

Basket. Four distinct rose sprays in each of the four corners of the bottom. Upturned corners with serrated edge. Single round handle is flattened on top and embossed with a distinctive pattern. 9" diameter x 5" high. Unmarked. **$5.00**

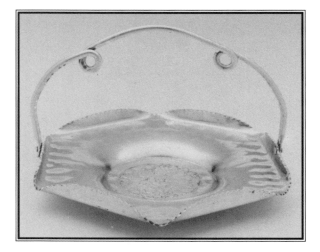

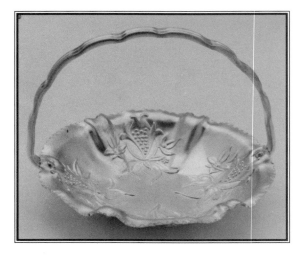

Basket. Hexagon shaped with round flower and fruit design in bottom. Upturned edges are serrated. Single round handle has double inside loops. 10" diameter x 6" tall. Hallmark: 6 (Cromwell). **$5.00**

Basket. Stylized flower design. Highly decorative with serrations on fluted edge. Single handle with indentations. Unmarked. **$5.00**

Basket. Tulip patterned hexagon basket. Serrated edge. Handle with cutouts has dogwood-type flowers on it. A nice added touch is the original tag, "Creations by Rodney Kent." 7" diameter x 4" tall. Hallmark: 16B (Rodney Kent). **$35.00**

Basket. Chrysanthemum pattern in "saddlebag" configuration of basket. Hammered background. Slight serrations on edge. Single strap handle. 11" long x 7" wide x 3" tall. Hallmark: 5A (Continental Silver). **$25.00**

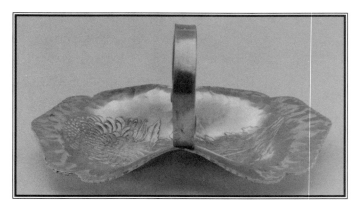

Basket. Has china insert in the Indian Tree pattern. Aluminum has rose pattern. Single handle has floral pattern. China is marked Farber and Shlevin. 7" diameter x 6" tall. Aluminum unmarked. **$35.00**

Basket. Wild rose pattern. Serrated edge on bowl. Single round handle is hammered. 6" diameter x 4" tall. Hallmark: 5C (Continental Silver). **$25.00**

Basket. Fruit and flower design with double inside loop handle. 11" diameter x 11" tall. Unmarked. **$5.00**

Basket. Palms design. Strap has square handle with round finials inserted at top of handle which looks like it would turn on the rivets. 10" diameter x 5" tall. Hallmark: 9B (Everlast). **$10.00**

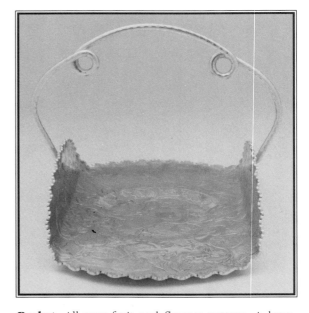

Basket. Fruit and flowers design. Double round handle is twisted with a square knot at the top. 10" diameter x 9" tall. Hallmark: 6 (Cromwell). **$10.00**

Basket. All-over fruit and flowers pattern. A long open ended basket is usually described as a flower cutting basket as flowers could be laid out full length as they were cut. The length certainly upholds that description here. Double inside loop handle. 14" long x 9" wide x 9" tall. Hallmark: 29 (Hand Finished). **$10.00**

Basket. Rose pattern. Beautiful design in the pattern which runs up into two panels on opposite sides. The sides where the single, round, floral designed handle is attached is highly fluted. Crimped edge all around. 9" long x 5" wide x 4" tall. Hallmark: 10 (Farber & Shlevin). **$3.00**

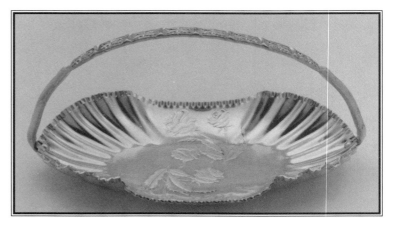

Basket. Chrysanthemum pattern "saddlebag" basket. Single strap handle has applied leaves, crimped edge. Similar to the one bottom page 36, except this is of nicer workmanship which includes the decorated handle. 11" long x 7" wide x 3" tall. Hallmark: 5A (Continental Silver). **$35.00**

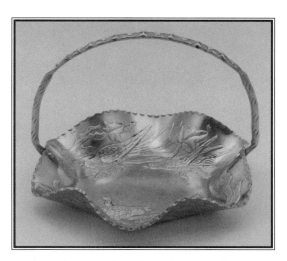

Basket. Flower and leaf band around edge. Single handle slips at end to be riveted to rim which is fluted and serrated. 9" diameter x 6" tall. Hallmark: 9B (Everlast). **$10.00**

Basket. Flying and perching birds similar to parrots on floral branch. Round decorated handle. 8" long x 7 wide x 5" tall. Hallmark: 10 (Farber & Shlevin). **$5.00**

Basket. Bowl is hammered and has serrated edge. Feet are applied leaves. Handle is open work with four-petal flowers similar to dogwood blossoms. 4" diameter x 4" tall. Unmarked. **$15.00**

Basket. Highly detailed angel fish with plant fronds. Hammered background looks like fish scales. Shallow lip turns back on self in serrated flutes. Double round handle has square knot at top. A beautiful piece! 12" diameter x 7" tall. Hallmark: 15B (Hand Forged). **$30.00**

Basket. Morning glory pattern basket with china insert which has the compote with fruit and flowers. Widely spaced serration on edge. Single handle has double loops to the outside. 11" diameter x 7" tall. Hallmark: 11 (Farberware). **$65.00**

Basket. Hammered with beaded rim. Double round handle has four twists on each side of finger hold. 9" diameter x 5" tall. Hallmark: 3B (Buenilum). **$5.00**

Basket. Acorn pattern. These acorns are teamed up with some beautifully detailed leaves which do not look like oak leaves. I suppose this is artistic license in practice. Unusual braided handle. Lip on bowl rolls under. 12" long x 8" wide x 10" tall. Hallmark: 5A (Continental Silver). **$25.00**

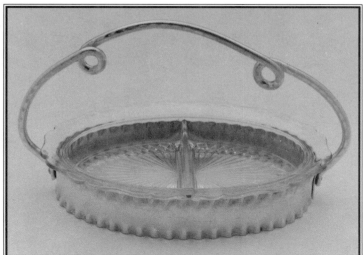

Basket. Rose pattern on aluminum. Has removable three part divided glass insert. Single round handle has molded twist pattern across the top. 7" diameter x 4" tall. Unmarked. **$10.00**

Basket. Consists of fluted metal holder with handle which accommodates a removable two part divided glass insert with fluted lip. Single round handle has double inside loops. 9" diameter x 6" tall. Unmarked. **$10.00**

Basket. Wild rose pattern. Corners are flat while sides are turned up in scalloped and fluted pattern. Single strap handle separates into tails which attach to rivets. Top of handle turns up on each side to form a slot in top. 10" long x 6" wide x 6" tall. Hallmark: 5B (Continental Silver). **$35.00**

Beverage Set. Tray with handle and 8 tumblers. 13" long. No mark. **$35.00**

Beverage server. Plain except for two sets of concentric circles running around the bottle. 5" diameter x 11" tall. Hallmark: 43B (Kromex). **$25.00**

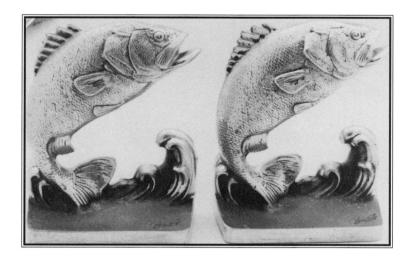

Bookends. Leaping bass with water sprays. Fine, fine detail. 5" long x 3" wide x 7" tall. Signed Bruce Cox on lower right hand corner of each piece. Hallmark: 48A. **$185.00**

Wooden Salad Server, Letter Opener, and Bookmark. Left is a wooden salad fork with hammered aluminum plate decoration of dogwood. Unmarked. Next is a fork and spoon salad server set. Pieces are wood with aluminum handles in the bamboo pattern. Unmarked. To right of center is a letter opener advertising a Kansas City bank. 8" long. Unmarked. Last on the right is a bookmark with a dog and cat. 8" long x ½" wide. Hallmark: 42B (DeMarsh Forge). Fork, **$10.00**; Salad Set, Pair **$30.00**; Letter opener, **$5.00**; Bookmark, **$20.00**

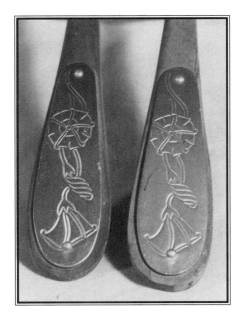

Wooden Salad Servers. This set has applied yellow anodized aluminum plates of the morning glory pattern. Total length is 9¾". Plate is 3³⁄₁₆" log. Unmarked. **$24.00**

Bowl. Dogwood pattern all-over. Has fluted, crimped rim. 7" diameter x 2" deep. Hallmark: 2A (Wendell August Forge). **$25.00**

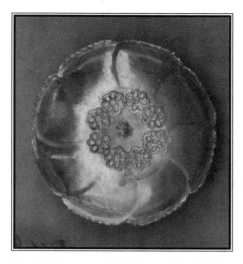

Bowl. Seven-petal daisy pattern in bottom with sides of bowl impressed resemble eight flower petals. Rim is scalloped and serrated. 6½" diameter x 1" deep. Hallmark: 3B (Buenilum). **$5.00**

Bowls. Left has a heavy grape pattern on hammered background. 9" diameter x 1½" deep. Unmarked. Right is a bowl with flamingos. Under the flamingos is a banner which reads "FLORIDA." 8½" diameter x 2½" deep. Hallmark: 40 (Burger). Left, **$5.00**; Right, **$5.00**

Bowl. Chrysanthemum pattern. Fluted edge. 5½" diameter x 1" deep. Hallmark: 5C (Continental Silver). **$25.00**

Bowl. Salad bowl with wheat pattern. 14" diameter x 4" deep. Hallmark: 21 (Palmer-Smith). **$65.00**

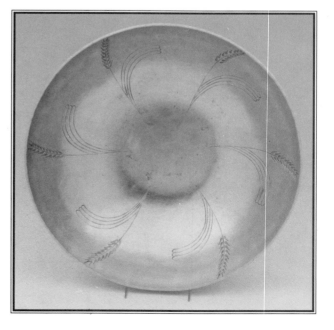

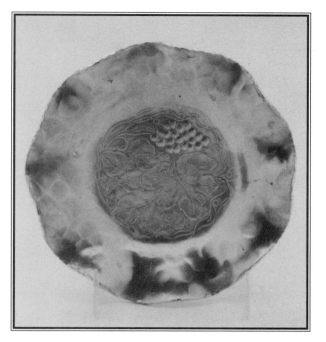

Bowl. Grape and vine pattern. Scalloped serrated edge. 6" diameter x 1" deep. Hallmark: 53 (H. Mansfield). **$5.00**

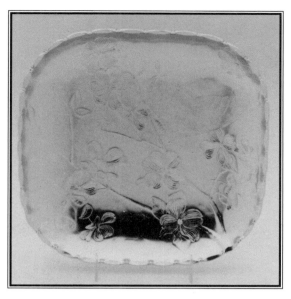

Bowl. Square bowl with dogwood and butterfly pattern. Gold anodized. Edge is ribbon and bead pattern. 8" square x 1" deep. Hallmark: 1A (Arthur Armour). **$45.00**

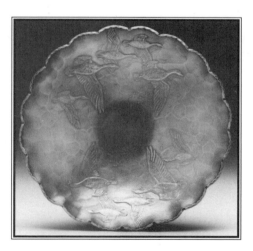

Bowl. Ducks. 10" diameter. Hallmark: 2B (Wendell August). **$65.00**

Bowl. Footed bowl in tulip pattern has two "eared" handles. Serrated edge on bowl. Crimped edge on foot. Ears are question mark shaped and attached only at lower end. Floral design. 10" diameter x 2" tall. Hallmark: 16A (Rodney Kent). **$45.00**

Footed bowl. Chrysanthemum with webbing pattern. Serrated edge on bowl. Beaded edge on foot. 9" diameter x 4" tall. Unmarked. **$25.00**

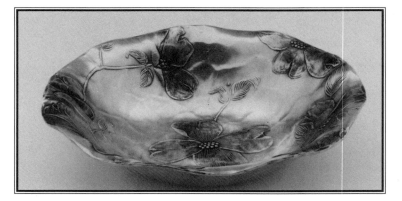

Bowl. Dogwood pattern. Plain fluted edge. 7" diameter x 2" deep. Hallmark: 2A (Wendell August Forge). **$45.00**

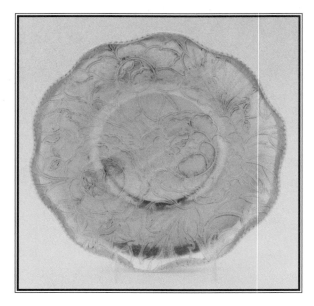

Bowl. Spun aluminum without decoration. Base 6½" flared to 11" diameter. Rim is 3½" deep. Hallmark: 30 (Kensington). **$15.00**

Bowl. All-over pattern of large flowers similar to cabbage rose. Fluted serrated edge. 8" diameter x 1" deep. Hallmark: 24B (Wilson Metal). **$5.00**

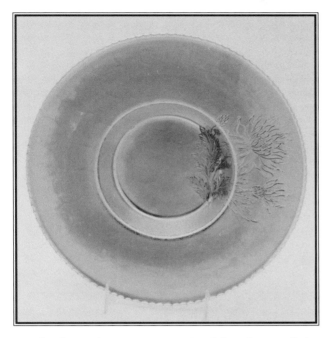

Bowl. Probably a cracker and dip tray. Beaded edge. Insert not original but certainly contemporary. 11¾" diameter. Hall: 3B (Buenilum) but lacks the words "Made in U.S.A." **$10.00**

Bowl. Chrysanthemum pattern. Bowl has deep well in center. Serrated edge. 9" diameter x 1" deep. Hallmark: 12A (Federal Silver). **$15.00**

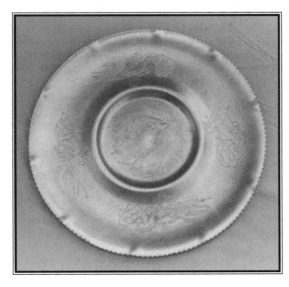

Bowl. Orchid-type flower. Serrated rim. 12" diameter x 2" deep. Hallmark: 27B (Federal). **$5.00**

Bowl. All-over hammered pattern with rim which is serrated. Carrying handle on each side consists of two aluminum wires coiled into three loops. 12" diameter x 2" deep. Hallmark: 3A Buenilum **$5.00**

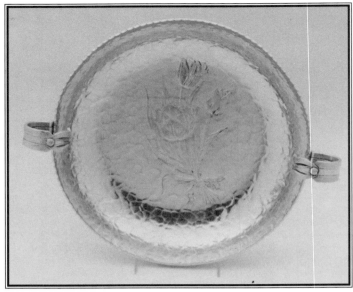

Bowl. Bamboo pattern. Faint serration on rim. 8" diameter x 1" deep. Hallmark. 9C (Everlast). **$10.00**

Bowl. Tulip pattern on hammered background. Eared handles have stylized tulip where attached. 10" diameter x 3" deep. Hallmark: 16A (Rodney Kent). **$35.00**

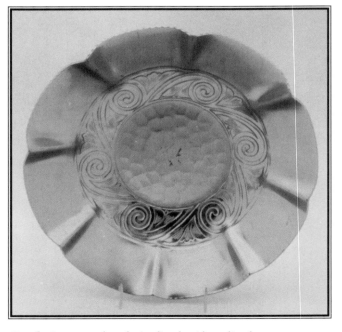

Bowl. Pine cone and needles design. Serrated rim. 10" diameter x 2" deep. Hallmark: 9C (Everlast). **$5.00**

Bowl. Copper-colored anodized with stylized wave or geometric design. Fluted edge. 11" diameter x 2" deep. Hallmark: 18 (Kraftware). **$10.00**

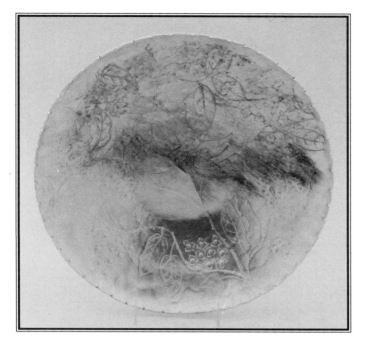

Bowl. Bittersweet pattern. Notched rim. 5" diameter x 1" deep. Hallmark: 2A (Wendell August Forge). **$35.00**

Bowl. Chrysanthemum pattern. Pinched flute edge with serrated rim. Applied leaf handles. 7" diameter x 1" deep. Hallmark: 5A (Continental Silver). **$25.00**

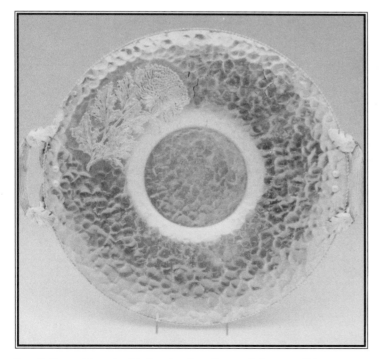

Bowl. Footed bowl with bracket handles and deep well in center. Chrysanthemum pattern. Beaded rim. Handles have applied leaves and are foliage embossed. 10" diameter x 4½" deep. Hallmark: 5A (Continental Silver). **$25.00**

Bowl. Chrysanthemum pattern. Applied leaf handles. Serrated rim. 7¼" diameter x 1½" deep. Hallmark: 5C (Continental). **$25.00**

Bowl. Bittersweet pattern. Notched rim. 11" diameter x 2" deep. Hallmark: 45C (DePonceau). **$35.00**

Bowl. Wild rose pattern with geometric pattern in well. Upturned, finely scalloped rim. 11" diameter x 3" deep. Hallmark: 5C (Continental). **$25.00**

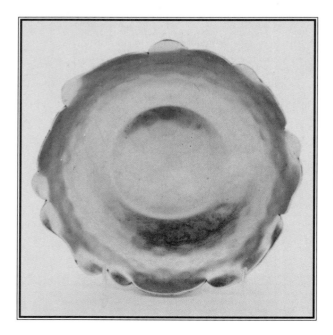

Bowl. Hammered effect with unevenly scalloped edge. 6" diameter x 1½" deep. Hallmark: 39B (McClelland Barclay). **$5.00**

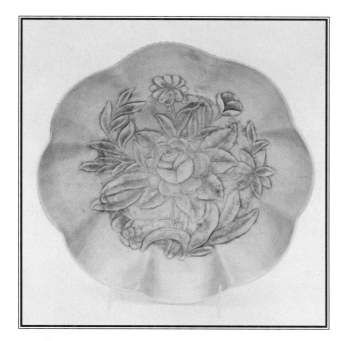

Bowl. All-over flowers and vines resemble trumpet vine. Nicely fluted edge. 7" diameter x 1" deep. Hallmark: 33 (Hand wrought). **$5.00**

Bowl. Mixed blossoms and foliage with a single large flower in the forefront. Scalloped and fluted rim. 11" diameter x 2½" deep. Hallmark: 34 (Warranted). **$5.00**

Bowls. Scenic pine pattern. Gold anodized. Largest is 11" long x 9" wide x 2" deep. Middle size is 9" long x 6" wide x 2" deep. The smallest is 5" diameter x 1" deep. Hallmark: 1A (Arthur Armour). Largest, **$35.00**; middle, **$25.00**; smallest, **$15.00**

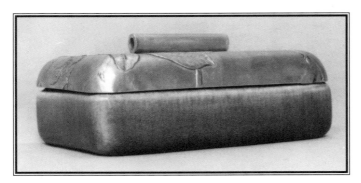

Box. Blue pottery bottom. Apple blossom pattern on lid which has a hollow tube handle on top. 5" long x 4" wide x 2½" deep. The metal top has the hallmark 2A (Wendell August Forge). **$90.00**

Breakfast Set. Lazy Susan base has an attached toast rack. There are two glass butter dishes with aluminum lids which have flower and leaf finials. There are also two glass jam jars with spoons. The aluminum lids have closed flower finials and a spoon slot. Unmarked. **$75.00**

Buffet Server. Tray is a rectangle of aluminum with ends rolled under to provide its own stand. Removable glass dishes are placed in single aluminum frame which is attached in the middle and has an eared handled on each end. Upright braces on dish frame are leaves. Lids have acorn pattern. 16" long x 7" wide x 5" tall. Hallmark: 5C (Continental). **$75.00**

Buffet Server. Footed single server has four-petal flowers on a ribbon for handles. The draped end of the ribbons form the four feet. Fitted, hammered lid with applied tulip and leaves finial. Very ornate. Hallmark: 16A (Rodney Kent) and 16B (Rodney Kent). **$35.00**

Butter Dishes. Note the different finishes. Left has a crown on each of the corners and a flower bud finial. 7" long x 4" wide x 3" tall. Hallmark: 41. The dish on the right has a scroll pattern with folded leaf finial. 7" long x 4" wide x 2" tall. Unmarked. **$8.00** each

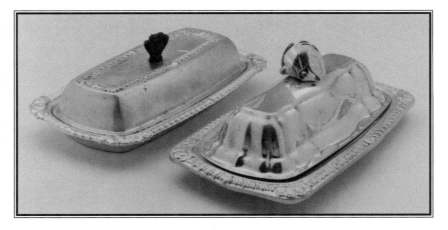

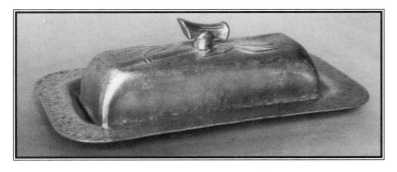

Butter Dish. Bamboo pattern with piece of bamboo as the finial. 7" long x 4" wide x 4" tall. Hallmark: 9C (Everlast). **$10.00**

Butter Dish and Napkin Rings. Chrysanthemum pattern butter dish with petal finial. Glass dish has wave-effect raised rim and star burst in bottom. Glass: 8¼" long x 4⅜" wide x ¾" deep. Lid: 7¼" long x 3³⁄₁₆" wide x 2⅜" deep. Unmarked. Free-form hand engraved napkin rings with flowers. Four "railroad tie" design lines around entire ring. Engraved "Rex" and "Susie" 1⅝" wide x 1⅝" tall. Unmarked. Butter Dish; **$10.00**; Napkin Rings, **$3.00** each

Cake Stand. A band of shields decoration. Serrated edge. 12" diameter x 8" tall. Hallmark: 24A (Wilson Metal). **$15.00**

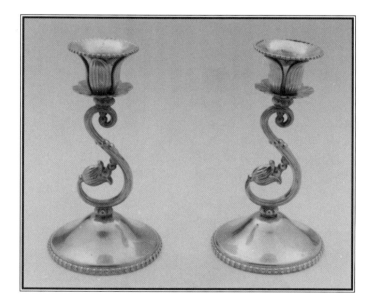

Candlesticks. "S" shaped with tulip. There are petals holding the candle well and beading around the base as well as the candle socket. This is a fine example of the silversmith at work when translating the art from silver to aluminum. Everything about this pair says, "First Class." 8" tall. Hallmark: II Faberware. **$45.00**

Candlesticks. Handled saucer with removable sockets. Another silver look-alike. Nice beading around edge. Wave effect on handle. Unmarked. **$20.00**

Candlesticks. Hammered effect with scalloped base and fluted bobache. 4" diameter x 3" tall. Hallmark: 9C (Everlast). **$20.00**

Candlesticks. Rectangular base, beaded rim. Curved handle on one side projects to a point out the other side after it goes under the candle socket. This technique is reminiscent of the old "betty lamps" which burned oil and could be put on the wall by jamming the pointed piece in between the logs or in the chinking in a log cabin. Hallmark: 3B (Buenilum). **$35.00**

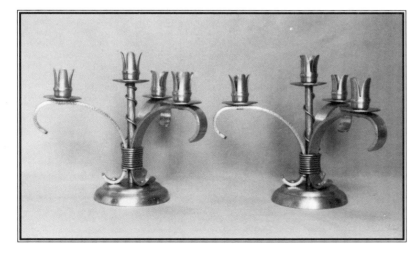

Candelabra. Hammered. Arms are riveted to the base then held against the upright by the wrapping of aluminum wire which extends to the very top. Cut-out. Sockets would accommodate a variety of candle sizes. Base 5" diameter. Candle arms approximately 10" diameter x 11". Unmarked. **$185.00**

Candelabra. Hammered into clean, simple lines with Art Nouveau influence. Base 6" square x 13" tall. Hallmark: 60 (Langbein). **$135.00**

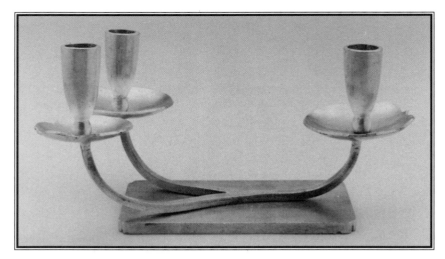

Candelabra. More of a primitive artist's feel here. Similar to what contemporary Middle Eastern artists are producing. Heavy hammered aluminum. 11" in length. Hallmark: 21 Palmer Smith **$85.00**

Candelabra and Hair Receiver. Hammered aluminum with three sockets. This shape is interesting as it feels as if it should have surrounded a central piece, such as a flower bowl. 21" long. Unmarked. All-over hair receiver hammered with a daisy on the side. Unmarked. Candelabra, **$65.00**; Hair Receiver, **$15.00**

Candleholder. Cast. Oak leaf and acorn. 10" long. Hallmark: 48 (Bruce Fox). **$45.00**

Candy Dish. Butterflies. Gold anodized. 12" long. Hallmark: Neocraft by Everlast. **$15.00**

Candy Dish. Center handle with two bowls. Pattern is a small daisy in a scroll-type leafy design. Fluted and serrated. 12" long x 6" wide. Unmarked. **$5.00**

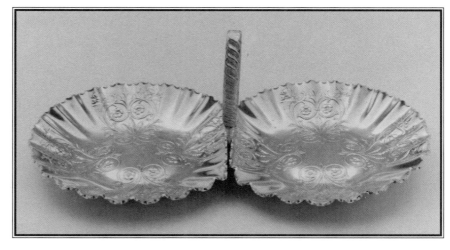

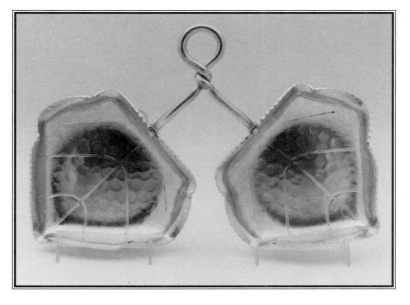

Candy Dish. Shaped like two leaves with the stems looped together to form the handle. Serrated edges. Leaves are 6" x 5". Hallmark: 3B (Buenilum). **$10.00**

Candy Dish. Bird and Grapes. 7½" x 13". Hallmark: Manning Bowman, Meriden, Conn., U. S. A. **$15.00**

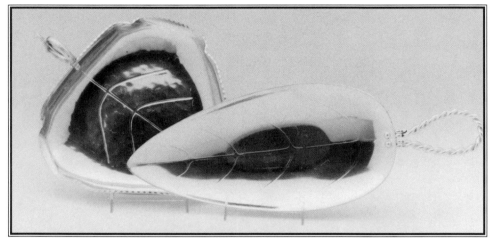

Candy Dishes. Leaf shaped and patterned. Long dish has flat twisted handle. Smooth edge. 15" long x 5" wide. Hallmark: 3C (Buenilum). Triangular shaped leaf has an ornate upright handle, serrated edge. It is 9" wide x 9" long x 2" tall. Hallmark: 3B (Buenilum). **$5.00** each

Candy Dish. Rose pattern. Double bowl with center handle. Fluted and serrated dishes. Rope motif stamped on handle. 16" long x 10" wide. Unmarked. **$5.00**

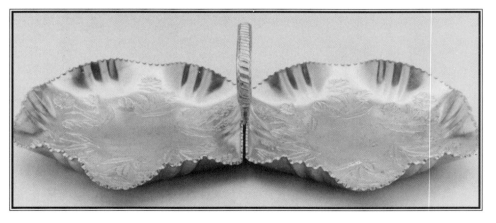

Candy Dish. All-over fruit and flower pattern. Coiled handle. Indentation provides three compartments in dish. Pie fluted edge. 9" diameter. Hallmark: 29 (Hand finished). **$5.00**

Candy Dish. Hammered effect. Large bead beaded rim. "S" shaped handle with tulip finial inside loop. 8" wide (9½" including handle) x 1¾" tall. Hallmark: II Faberware. **$10.00**

Candy Dishes. Tulip spray design. Round dish has indentation to form two sides in bowl. Single cord handle. 7" diameter. Unmarked. Double dish with center handle. 8" long x 5" wide. Unmarked. **$5.00** each

Candy Dish. Round fruit and flowers design. Nice deep round bowls have pattern in bottom only. Finely fluted edges on bowl. Center handle forms large loop. 13" long x 7" wide. Hallmark: 6 (Cromwell). **$10.00**

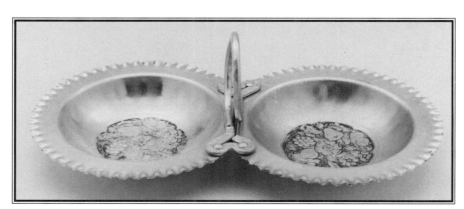

Candy Dishes. Left is a rose pattern. Double dish. Central handle. Fluted sides. Serrated rim. 13" long x 7" wide. Unmarked. Right is also the rose pattern with fluted sides and serrated rim. There is a difference in the handle pattern and the size, which is 9" long x 6" wide. Marked: Thames Japan. **$5.00** each

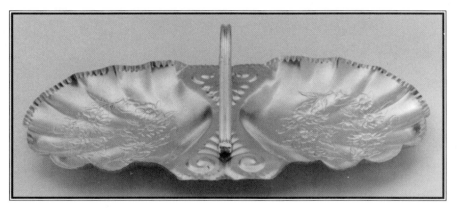

Candy Dish. Double with center handle. Daisy pattern. Fluted sides with crimped rim. 9" long x 5" wide. Unmarked. **$5.00**

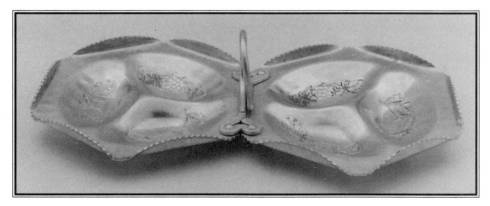

Candy Dish. Two bowls with center handle, but that's as far as the similarity to other center handled bowls goes. These bowls have indentations to form three compartments, each of which has a fruit panel. The rims on the hexagon shaped dishes are turned up and serrated. Looped handle. 15" long x 9" wide. Hallmark: 6 (Cromwell). **$10.00**

Candy Dish. China inserts in Indian Tree pattern. Rose pattern on aluminum edges. Center handle has floral embossing. 12" long x 7" wide. China marked Faber and Sheavin, Inc. No hallmark on metal. **$45.00**

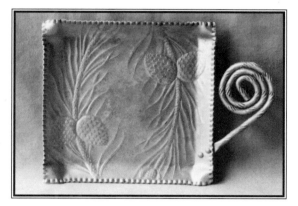

Candy Dish. Pine cone and needles pattern. Square with upturned edge and crimped rim. Handle is single coil of aluminum. 6" square dish. Unmarked. **$5.00**

Candy Dish. Leaf shaped dish has a three-masked sailing ship design. Tall handle with curlicue on end. 8" long x 6" wide x 7" tall. Hallmark: 22A (World Hand Forged). **$25.00**

Casserole Holder. There is a wheat pattern with panels of different vegetables. On the front in the photo are pea pods, to the right are beets, and to the left is an ear of corn. Four feet, two of which extend up the side into handles. Heavy, stylized finial; lid cut to accommodate handled glass insert. 8" diameter x 6" tall. Unmarked. **$25.00**

Casserole. Bamboo pattern with pieces of bamboo assembled to form handles and finial. Lid cut to accommodate handled glass insert. 7" diameter x 5" tall. Hallmark: 9C (Everlast). **$10.00**

Casserole. Bamboo pattern with bamboo finial. No handles. Lid fits inside of base. 7" diameter x 4" tall. Hallmark: 9C (Everlast). **$10.00**

Casserole. Hammered with beaded edges and beaded circle on lid. Finial is a double loop tipped with beads and a tapered end. Lid fits inside base. 8" diameter x 6" tall. Hallmark: 3B (Buenilum). **$5.00**

Casserole. Flower band on lid. Flower and leaf finial. Lid cut to accommodate handled glass insert. Hammered base with "D" bracket handles. Hallmark: 9B (Everlast). **$5.00**

Casserole. Flower band on lid. Ball and leaf finial. Lid cut to accommodate handled glass insert. Hammered base. 10" diameter x 5" tall. Hallmark: 9B (Everlast). **$5.00**

Casserole. Flower and leaf band pattern. Flower finial. Hammered base. Embossed handle. Lid cut to accommodate handled glass insert, which is shown in photo. 9" diameter x 4" high. Hallmark: 9B (Everlast). **$5.00**

Casserole. Rose pattern. Overlapping rose petal finial with leaves. No handles. Lid overlaps base. 8" diameter x 4" tall. Hallmark: 22B (World Hand Forged). **$5.00**

Casserole. Tomato pattern. Flat topped flower and leaf finial. Lid fits inside base. 9" diameter x 5" tall. Hallmark: 9C (Everlast). **$5.00**

Casserole. All-over hammered effect with notched rims on top and bottom. Of special note are the finial and the three feet. They contain marbles. The finial is comprised of four square tabs which grasp the marble, and there are four tabs laying against the lid as with the leaf effect. The feet have the same tab arrangement grasping marbles. Ribbon type handles on either side have the same design as the tabs on the finial and feet. Lid sits atop base. 6" diameter x 4" tall. Unmarked. **$10.00**

Casserole. Hammered effect. Tulip finial with ribbons underneath. Lid overlaps base. 8" diameter x 6" tall. Hall-mark: 16 B (Rodney Kent). **$10.00**

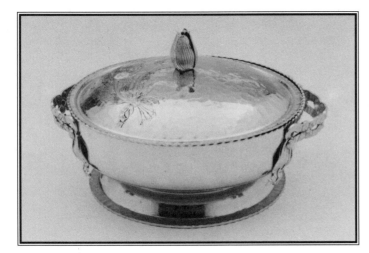

Casserole. Tulip spray pattern on top. Bottom has a base. Tulip bloom finial. Open-work handles have four petal flowers across handle with ribbons at each end. Lid sits atop base. 8" diameter x 6" tall. Unmarked. **$10.00**

Casserole. Hammered, but pattern is concentric circles around the top. Handles are hanging rings. Finial is a wire loop. Base tapers to a relatively small bottom. Lid fits inside base. 8" diameter x 6" tall. Marked: Vasco Italy. **$2.00**

Casserole. Round fruit and flower pattern around finial. Lid sits atop base. Handles are 1½" circles of round wire. Small, button finial. 7" diameter x 3" tall. Hallmark: 6 (Cromwell). **$3.00**

Casserole. Pea vine pattern. Has a pea pod finial atop lid that fits down inside base. 7" diameter x 4" tall. Hallmark: 9E (Everlast). **$15.00**

Casserole. Dogwood and butterfly pattern. Lid cut to accommodate handled glass insert, which is shown in photo. Moveable ring finial. Lipped handles. 10" diameter x 4" tall. Hallmark: 1A (Arthur Armour). **$50.00**

Casserole Holder. An armada of ships sails around the entire exterior. Clip-type handles are open at the bottom. Crimped design on top edge. 9" diameter x 3" tall. Hallmark: 28B (Forman). **$5.00**

Casserole. Bottom is plain. Lid is hammered effect. Moveable ring handles. Finial is black and white and stands up on a stem. Lid overlaps base. 9" diameter x 6" tall. Hallmark: 36B (Neocraft). **$3.00**

Buffet Server or Bun Warmer. Smooth finish. Exaggerated "S" shaped legs with tulip inserts. Foot design is reproduced in the finial. Lid fits snugly inside base. 9" diameter x 8" tall. Hallmark: II Faberware. **$25.00**

Casserole. Floral band pattern. Rolled handles. 11" wide x 3¼" deep. Bowl is 9" diameter x 2¼" deep. Hallmark: 9B (Everlast) with rounded ends on border. **$5.00**

Fondue Pot. Beaded lip. Detail on Sterno cup and base. Wood handle. Whole is 6¾" tall. Pot is 5¼" diameter x 3" deep x 11" wide (including handle). Hallmark: 3C (Buenilum) **$5.00**

Cigarette Box. Bittersweet. 3" x 5" x 1½". Hallmark: 2B (Wendell August). **$75.00**

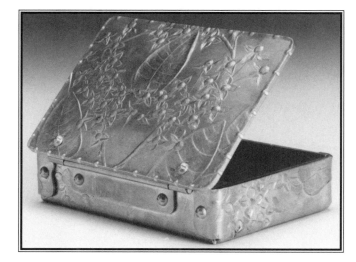

Cigarette Box. Cast. Duck figure applied. 3" x 5" x 1½". Hallmark: 59 (Laird Argental). **$75.00**

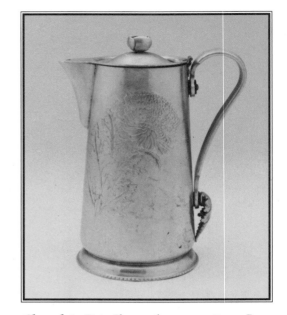

Chocolate Pot. Chrysanthemum pattern. Base is beaded on bottom. Lid with overlapping petal finial is hinged to pot. Handle has applied flower at bottom. 5" diameter x 10" tall. Hallmark: 5A (Continental). **$85.00**

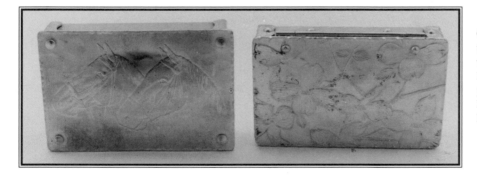

Cigarette Boxes. Left has pattern of two horse's heads on top. 5½" long x 4" wide x 1½" deep. Hallmark: 22B (World Hand Forged). Right is the dogwood pattern. 5½" long x 3½" wide x 1" deep. Hallmark: 2A (Wendell August Forge). Left, **$65.00**; Right, **$75.00**

Cigarette Box. Pine cone and needle pattern. 5⅜" long x 3⅜" wide x 1⅔" tall. Hallmark: 63 (Town). **$75.00**

Coaster Sets. Right is the five petal flower pattern. Eight coasters in a trivet-type holder. Coasters are 3½" diameter. Hallmark: 9C (Everlast). On the left is the bamboo pattern. Eight coasters in a trivet-type holder. Coasters are 3½" diameter. Hallmark: 9C (Everlast). **$20.00** each

Coaster Set. Chrysanthemum pattern. Twelve coasters in a basket-type holder. Handle has applied leaves at each end. Coasters are 4" diameter. Hallmark: 5A (Continental). **$30.00**

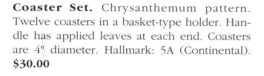

Coaster Set. Bamboo pattern. Four coasters in a trivet type holder. Coasters are 3½" diameter. Hallmark: 9C (Everlast). **$20.00**

Coaster Set. Tulip blossom pattern wherein coasters are actually shaped like the blossom. Seven coasters in basket type holder with open-work ribbon handles. Original tag stating, "Creations of Rodney Kent." Unmarked on metal. **$35.00**

Coaster Set. Four coasters in walnut holder. Scenic patterns, all different. Shown are a scene of Pittsburgh and wild turkeys. Very good detail. 3" diameter. Hallmark: 2C (Wendell August Forge). **$50.00**

Coasters. Left is a set of eight coasters in a holder, decorated with a concentric spiral. Held in a dish-rack type tray. 3" diameter. Hallmark: 9C (Everlast). On the right is a coaster with a bird on a branch. 5" diameter. Hallmark: 45C (DePonceau). Coaster set, **$10.00**; Coaster, **$20.00**

Coasters. Left is an angel fish pattern. 5" diameter. Unmarked. Right is the flying ducks pattern. 4" diameter. Hallmark: 9B (Everlast). Left, **$5.00**; Right, **$5.00**

Coasters. Left is a jumping marlin pattern. 5" diameter. Hallmark: 2A (Wendell August Forge). Right is the Capitol building in Washington, D.C. 4½" diameter. Marked: Alpha Swiss. Left, **$15.00**; Right, **$3.00**

Coasters. Left is the top view of a beetle, and right is the side view of cricket. 3½" diameter. Hallmark: 2F (Wendell August Forge). **$35.00** each

Coasters. Left is a fox hunter on horseback with hounds. Right is a heavy grape pattern. 5" diameter. Hallmark on fox hunter: 9B (Everlast). Grape is unmarked. Left, **$5.00**; Right, **$3.00**

Coasters. Aluminum shell with a glass liner over a print in the bottom. Shown are a jumping bass and woodcocks. Beaded rims. 5" diameter. Unmarked. **$5.00** each

Coasters. Hammered effect aluminum cap over the rim of glass coaster with sunburst design in bottom. Set of eight shown. 4½" diameter. Unmarked. **$3.00** each

Coaster. Three flying ducks against a background of cat-tails and water. 5" diameter. Unmarked. **$2.00**

Coasters. Left is a heron pattern; center is a parrot pattern; right is a butterfly pattern. 3½" diameter. Unmarked. **$2.00** each

Coaster Set. One mountain lion, one duck, and two turkeys. 3" diamener. Hallmark: 2C (Wendell August). **$45.00**

Coaster Set. One dogwood, one holly, and two pine cones. 3" diameter. Hallmark: 2C (Wendell August). **$30.00**

Coaster Set in Display Box. Five petal flowers. Hallmark: 9B (Everlast). **$25.00**

Coaster. Left is a sailboat with rope design around edge of base. Slight fluting on rim. 3¹³/₁₆" diameter. Right is a sitting Scottie dog. 3⅜" diameter. Both are unmarked. **$3.00** each

The following two pages are **coasters**, some of which are commonly found, some of which are rare. All coasters are unmarked unless otherwise noted. **Row 1**: Goose, **$10.00**; pine cone and needles, **$2.00**; peony flower, **$2.00**; tulip flower, **$2.00**. **Row 2**: Two flying ducks with cat-tails, marked Hand Wrought, **$2.00**; oak leaves and acorns, marked Westbend blue anodized, **$2.00**; daisy type flower, **$2.00**; water lily, **$5.00**. **Row 3**: Two flying ducks, **$5.00**; single flying duck, **$4.00**; gold anodized leaf, **$5.00**; round floral and fruit pattern, **$2.00 Row 4**: Rose blossom with five-petal flower, **$2.00**; flying ducks and cat-tails, **$2.00**; pine cone and needles, Hallmark: 2C (Wendell August Forge), **$6.00**; swimming swans, **$5.00**. **Row 5**: Pansy, **$2.00**; cat-tails with flying ducks in background, **$2.00**; pine cone and needles, **$6.00**; heron, **$6.00**.

Row 1: Assorted fruit, **$2.00**; roses, Hallmark: 9C (Everlast), **$2.00**; bird dog on point, **$5.00**; daisy, Hallmark: 9B (Everlast), **$2.00**. **Row 2**: Fruit and flowers, Hallmark: 9B (Everlast), **$2.00**; heavy grape, Hallmark: 9B (Everlast), **$2.00**; poinsettia, gold anodized, **$5.00**; five-petal flower, **$2.00**. **Row 3**: "E," **$2.00**; Reynolds Metals logo, **$2.00**; dancing mule and sheep, **$2.00**; rose, **$2.00**. **Row 4**: Christopher Columbus's ship, Hallmark: 9B (Everlast), **$8.00**; stylized figure, **$3.00** four-petal dogwood, **$4.00**; floral, Hallmark: 9B (Everlast), **$4.00**. **Row 5**: Scotty dog, **$8.00**; "S," **$2.00**; four-petal dogwood Hallmark: 1C (Arthur Armor) **$8.00**; five petal flower, **$5.00**.

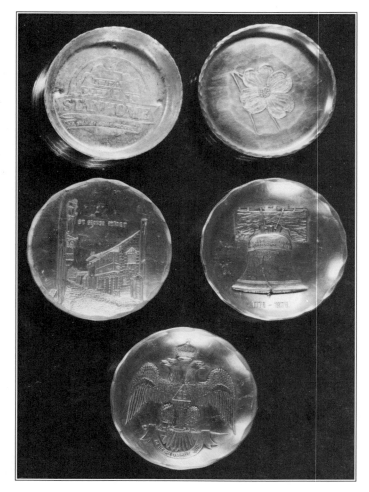

Coasters. Top left, Stanhome logo of Stanley Home Products. Unmarked. Top right is a five-petal flower. Hallmark: 2A (Wendell August Forge). Middle left is Street Scene "St. George Street." Hallmark: 2D (Wendell August Forge). Middle right is liberty bell. Hallmark: 2E (Wendell August Forge). Bottom is armorial figure of double headed eagle with spread wings. There is a crown over the eagle. Ribbon at bottom says, "Deus Meumque Jus." Hallmark: 2C (Wendell August Forge). Stanhome logo, **$4.00**; Flower, **$5.00**; Street Scene, **$5.00**; Bell, **$5.00**; figure, **$10.00**

Coffee Urn. Chrysanthemum pattern. Handles have familiar leaf applied at the bottom. Glass finial on lid. Spigot at the bottom. 7" diameter at widest point x 15" tall. Marked: Continental Silver Company, Inc. **$85.00**

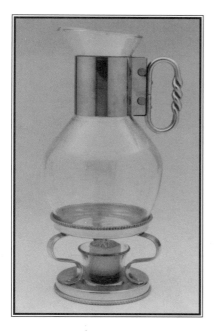

Coffee Server. Glass pot. Collar around neck has twisted handle. Beaded lip base has candle holder. No pattern. 17" tall. Unmarked. **$5.00**

Compote, covered. All-over hammered effect. Tulip and ribbon finial. Openwork ribbon stem. Hammered base. Unmarked. **$15.00**

Compote. Stylized flower design. Double wire curlicue stem on cone shape. 8" diameter x 5" tall. Unmarked. **$5.00**

Compote. Hammered effect. 6" diameter x 5" tall. Unmarked. **$10.00**

Compote. Wild rose pattern. 5" diameter x 5" tall. Hallmark: 5B (Continental). **$25.00**

Console Set. Consists of compote and matching pair of candleholders. Pine cone and needle pattern. Hallmark: 2A (Wendell August Forge). **$250.00**

Creamer and Sugar. All-over hammered effect. Lid on sugar has open flower finial with leaves. Two "elbow" handles on sugar, one creamer. Hallmark: 22B (World Hand Forged). **$5.00**

Creamer and Sugar. All-over hammered effect, fluted rims. No lid on sugar. Rounded handles. Unmarked. **$5.00**

Creamer and Sugar on Tray. Nice pitcher-shaped creamer with full circle handle. Finial on sugar lid is a double loop ending in a bead and a tapered tulip bulb end. Same end finish on tray handle. Hallmark: 3B (Buenilum). **$15.00**

Creamer and Sugar. Diagonal slash band around top of each. Curled aluminum rod handles. Creamer: 2¾" tall (3" including handle) x 3½" wide (4½" including handle). Sugar: 2¾" tall (3" including handle) x 3 ⅜" wide (5½" including handle). Both are unmarked. **$5.00**

Crumb Brush and Tray. Tulip pattern on tray. Tray handle and brush handle both have a six-petal flower and ribbon design. Unmarked. **$35.00**

Crumber and Tray. Leaf design. Hallmark: 9A (Everlast). **$5.00**

Crumb Brush and Tray. Grape vine pattern. Lucite brush handle. Plastic bristles. Hallmark: 9C (Everlast). **$10.00**

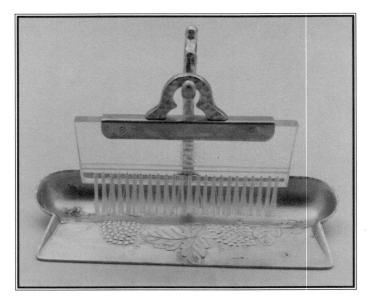

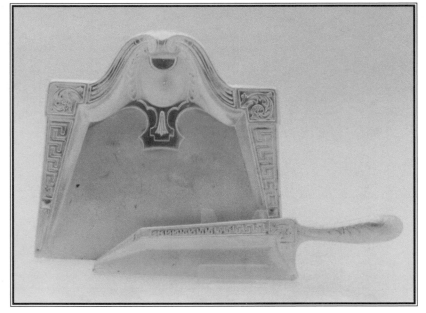

Crumber and Tray. Greek Key pattern. Unmarked. **$5.00**

Cups or Mugs. Hammered effect. Rolled lip. Ear handles. Copper colored. 3" diameter x 3" tall. Unmarked. **$1.00** each

Child's Cup and Collapsible Cup. Left is a child's cup with picture panels showing elephant and other animals. 5" diameter x 5" tall. Unmarked. On the right is a collapsible cup with handle. 5" diameter x 5" tall. Marked: Quaker State Standard. Child's Cup, **$10.00**; Collapsible Cup, **$5.00**

Collapsible Cup, Gravy Boat, Matchbox Cover, and Ice Tongs. Center is a collapsible cup with lid, a souvenir of Hot Springs, Arkansas. Unmarked. Top left is a gravy boat in the bamboo pattern. Top right is a cover for a kitchen matchbox in the acorn and oak leaf pattern. Hallmark: 2F (Wendell August Forge). Bottom right and left are ice tongs with hammered effect pattern. Unmarked. Collapsible Cup, **$5.00**; Gravy Boat, **$20.00**; Matchbox cover, **$35.00**; Ice Tongs, $**4.00** each

Child's Cup. Two "railroad tie" lines circle cup near top and bottom. Opposite side from handle is an engraved shield with stars and stripes and "St. Louis." Round handle. 1¾" diameter x 2³⁄₁₆" tall. Unmarked. **$5.00**

Children's Dishes. Left to right, front row: Cup, 2⅜" diameter x 2¾" tall. Marked: "Baby Sandy's Cup" Pat. Sept. 23, 1924. Hallmark: 64 (Perco); Cup and Saucer, nice old pieces. Very light weight. Saucer 4" diameter, cup 1¾" tall x 2⅛" diameter. Etched design. Unmarked. Band of animals around outside. 2¾" diameter x 1¾" tall. Unmarked; Wash Bowl, 5" diameter x 2" tall. Unmarked. Back row: Mugs, four engraved lines. 2⅜" diameter x 2½" tall. Marked: Swiss; Cup, "Baby" on front. 2⅝ diameter x ¾" tall; Cup, Panel with pony cart, clown and elephant around exterior. 3⅛" diameter x 2⅝" tall. Unmarked; Cup, **$20.00**; Cup & Saucer, **$12.00**; Bowl, **$10.00**; Wash bowl, **$8.00**; Mug, **$12.00**; Baby Cup, **$10.00**; Cup, **$8.00**

Child's Plate. Alphabet around edge. 7" diameter. Unmarked. **$30.00**

Cups. In rear are two collapsible cups, one with a sailboat on the lid, the other with a six point star. 2⅛" base flaring to 2⅝" diameter at top. 1¼" tall expandable to 2¾". Collapsible Cups, **$10.00** each; Nested Cups, **$15.00** set

Dip Server. Bamboo pattern on supporting rods and wheels. Dishes are hammered. 11" tall. Hallmark: 9C (Everlast). **$45.00**

Double Boiler. Highly polished. Wood handle and finial. Has Pyrex liner. 7" diameter. Hallmark: 3B (Buenilum). **$10.00**

Fruit Bowl and Knives. All-over fruit and flowers pattern. Loop wire handles. Serrated lip and base. 11" diameter x 4" tall. Unmarked. **$25.00**

Gravy Boat. Chrysanthemum pattern. 6" diameter x 3" tall. Hallmark: 5A (Continental). **$25.00**

Gravy Boat. Attached underplate. Highly polished; beaded lip and base rim. Bead and tapered end on wire handle. 6" diameter x 3" tall. Hallmark: 3B (Buenilum). **$20.00**

Hurricane Lamp. Double twisted handle. Double candle socket. 9" long x 10" tall. Hallmark: 3A (Buenilum). **$45.00**

Hurricane Lamps. Heavily embossed grape and leaf pattern. Circular finger hold with thumb support. 10" wide (including handle). Bowl is 8" wide x 3⅜" deep. Chimneys (not original) are 8½" tall with 3" bases. Hallmark: 9C (Everlast). **$45.00** pair

Hurricane Lamps. Heavily embossed grape and leaf pattern. Circular finger hold with thumb support. 10" wide (including handle). Bowl is 8" wide x 3⅜" deep. Chimneys (not original) are 8½" tall with 3" bases. Hallmark: 9C (Everlast). **$40.00** pair

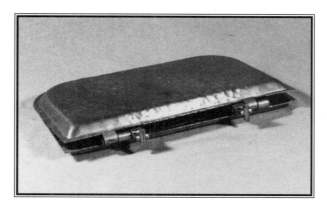

Folding Server. Branch with pine cones and needles pattern. Heavy hammered handled. Fluted edge. Folded tray is 11⅞" wide x 7½" long, including feet. Opened tray is 13⅝" long x 11⅞" wide x 5¼" tall to top of handle. Hallmark: 9C (Everlast) Marked: 1078. **$25.00**

Ice Bucket. Open, hammered effects. "Barbell" handles. Fluted top. 10" diameter x 5" tall. Hallmark: 9B (Everlast). **$15.00**

Ice Bucket. Open, hammered interior, beaded lip. Twisted handle with bead and tapered end decorations. 5" diameter x 6" tall. Hallmark: 3B Buenilum. **$10.00**

Ice Bucket. Covered. Highly polished. Wood finial. Finger-grip handles. 8" diameter x 9" tall. Hallmark: 20 (N. S. Co.). **$10.00**

Ice Bucket. Intaglio flowers. 7" diameter x 3" tall. Hallmark: 9A (Everlast). **$10.00**

Ice bucket. Hammered effect. Self opening by moving handle. 8" diameter x 8" tall. Unmarked. **$5.00**

Ice Bucket. Open. Acorn and leaf pattern. Cane-shaped handles. 7" diameter x 3" tall. Hallmark: 5C (Continental). **$15.00**

Ice Bucket. No pattern, but shaped like medieval helmet. 10" diameter x 16" tall. Mark: Made in Hong Kong. **$20.00**

Ice Bucket. Chrysanthemum pattern. Lid with mushroom and leaf finial fits down inside base. Ribbon handles. 8" diameter x 9" tall. Hallmark: 5A (Continental). **$40.00**

Ice Bucket. Tulip pattern. Flat ribbon decoration on lid, which is attached by a chain to the handle. When the handle is moved, the lid comes off. 8" diameter x 7" tall. Unmarked. **$40.00**

Ice Bucket. Hammered effect. Mushroom and leaf finial on lid which fits down into base. Heavy hammered handles. 9" diameter x 7" tall. Hallmark: 9E (Everlast). **$10.00**

Ice Bucket. Hammered effect. Black handles and finial. 8" diameter x 12" tall. Hallmark: 43B (Kromex). **$10.00**

Ice Bucket. Hammered effect, beehive shaped. Sling handle. Mushroom finial. 8" diameter x 8" tall. Unmarked. **$10.00**

Ice Bucket. Highly polished. Plain. Self-finialed lid fits squarely atop footed bucket. Ring handles. 7" diameter x 8" tall. Marked: Made in Italy. **$5.00**

Jelly Jar and Ladle. Blue pottery insert. Plate 5" diameter. Hallmark: Turnipyard, Deerfield, Mass. **$30.00**

Jelly Jar, Salt and Pepper Shakers, and Communion Cups. Left is a Jelly Jar of glass with a hammered aluminum lid with tulip bud finial. 3" diameter x 4" tall. Unmarked. Top right is a pair of salt and pepper shakers. Anodized copper on one and brass on the other. The smallest set of salt and pepper shakers I have seen in aluminum. Unmarked. 1⅞" tall. Bottom right is a pair of Communion Cups. 1" diameter x 1" tall. Unmarked. Jelly Jar, **$5.00**; Salt & Pepper, Shaker, **$10.00**; Communion Cups, **$2.00** each

Jelly Jar and Ladle. Underplate 5" diameter. Hallmark: Nekrassoff. **$35.00**

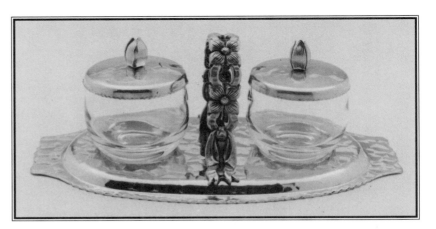

Jam and Jelly Server. It has the open work four-petal flower on ribbon handle. Tulip bud finials on the aluminum lids. 9" long x 5" wide. Unmarked. **$35.00**

Collection of Jewelry. Top left is a medallion showing a church. 2" diameter. Hallmark: 2C (Wendell August Forge). Top center is a medallion. Wild rose pattern. 2½" diameter. Unmarked. Top right is a bracelet, souvenir of the Grand Ole Opry. Unmarked. Bottom left is a bolo tie clasp with Indian signs. 2" long x ½" wide. Unmarked. Bottom right is a link bracelet in the pine cone pattern. Hallmark: 2A (Wendell August Forge). Church Medallion, **$25.00**; Flower Medallion, **$5.00**; C-type Bracelet, **$5.00**; Bolo clasp, **$5.00**; Link bracelet, **$50.00**

Collection of Jewelry. Top left is a C-type bracelet with stylized daisy and vine pattern. Unmarked. Top center C-Type bracelet says "Souvenir of New Caledonia." This was probably made by a soldier during World War II possibly from aluminum salvaged from a Japanese aircraft. Unmarked. Top right has a leaf pattern. Unmarked. Center left C-type bracelet is in the pine cone pattern. Hallmark: 2E (Wendell August Forge). Bottom row is a matching pendant on a link chain and link bracelet in the wild rose pattern. Unmarked. Floral bracelet, **$10.00**; Souvenir bracelet, **$15.00**; Leaf bracelet, **$10.00**; Pine cone bracelets, **$35.00** each; Pine cone broach, **$35.00**; Pendant, **$15.00**; Link bracelet, **$35.00**

Key chains. Left to right, top to bottom are a teddy bear, an owl, a palm tree, a light house, two deer, and a squirrel. Hallmark: 42 A (DeMarsh Forge). **$12.00** each

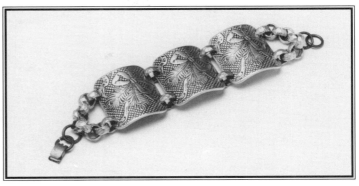

Bracelet. No Mark. **$25.00.**

Money Clips. Left to right, top to bottom are a light house, teddy bear, butterfly, strawberry, teddy bear, and butterfly. Hallmark: 42A (DeMarsh Forge). **$12.00**

Lazy Susan. Tulip spray pattern. Six-petal flower on ribbon decoration on two sides. 18" diameter. Hallmark: 16A (Rodney Kent). **$15.00**

Lazy Susan. Fruit and flower pattern. Serrated edge. 16" diameter. Hallmark: 6 (Cromwell). **$5.00**

Lazy Susan. Acorn pattern. Open flower and leaf decoration on two sides of plate. 18" diameter. Unmarked. **$15.00**

Lazy Susan. Ivy vine pattern. Upturned strap loop handles have an applied leaf. Another deep-walled piece. 13" diameter. Unmarked. **$10.00**

Lazy Susan. All-over fruit and flower pattern with one butterfly. Welled for glass insert. 14" diameter x 3" tall. Unmarked. **$12.00**

Tiered Lazy Susan. Tulip spray pattern. 11" diameter x 10" tall. Unmarked. **$15.00**

Tiered Lazy Susan. Fruit and flower pattern. 12" diameter x 13" tall. Hallmark: 6 (Cromwell). **$10.00**

Letter Basket. World map pattern. Inside gold anodized, outside silver anodized. 7" long x 5" wide x 6" tall. Hallmark: 1A (Arthur Armour). **$175.00**

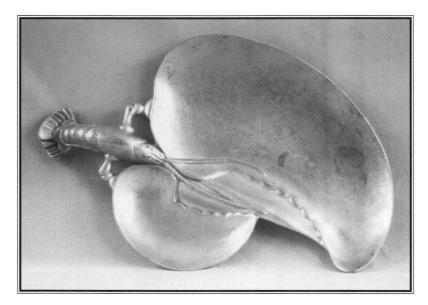

Tray. Bowl section become enlarged pincers for lobster handle. 15" long x 11" wide. Hallmark: 48 (Bruce Fox). **$35.00**

Fish Dish. Wonderful detail. 18¾" long x 8⅛" wide. Hallmark: 48 (Bruce Fox) Hallmark: Royal Hickman RH8. **$85.00**

Detail of Bruce Fox Hallmark on fish dish.

Magazine Rack. Embossed flying ducks, cat-tails, and an island. This is a solid piece of aluminum going from one handle down and around to the other. There are braces near the top at each end. 14" long x 9" wide x 9" tall. Hallmark: 2C (Wendell August Forge). **$250.00**

Magazine Rack. Swan. 14" long x 8" wide at bottom x 18" to top of handle. Hallmark: 2C (Wendell August). **$350.00**

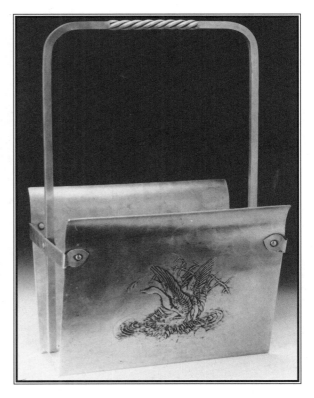

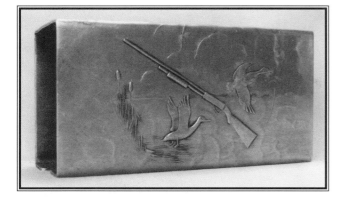

Kitchen match box cover. Shotgun with flying ducks pattern. Hallmark: 2A (Wendell August Forge). **$75.00**

Match Box Covers. Left is pinecone, and right is bittersweet. Both hallmark: 2C (Wendell August). **$65.00 each**

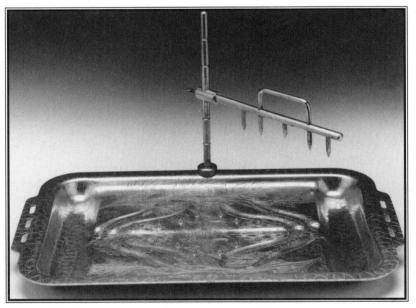

Meat Server. Chrysanthemum. 18" x 14". Hallmark: 28A (Forman Family). **$20.00**

Mint Dish with glass insert. Left, Dogwood pattern. 12" diameter. Hallmark: 2A (Wendell August Forge). **$45.00**

Mint Dish. Right, Chrysanthemum pattern. Pansy shaped dish is molded into three compartments. Has center open-flower finial. Impressed edge detail. 10" diameter. Unmarked. **$20.00**

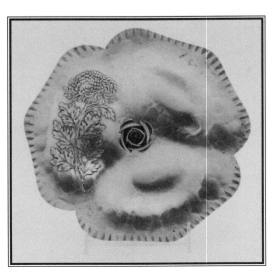

Napkin Holder. Homemade of two pieces of decorated aluminum nailed to a base of wood. Hammered background. Outline of design and initial "F" is made by placing a nail on the aluminum and tapping to make an indentation. A nice handicraft piece. 6" long x 3" wide and 3" tall. **$10.00**

Napkin Holder. Thistle pattern. Crimped edge. 6" long x 2" wide x 4" tall. Unmarked. **$10.00**

Napkin Holder. Flower and ribbon pattern. Stands up on four leaf-shaped legs. 6" long x 2" wide x 3½" tall. Unmarked. **$15.00**

Napkin Holder. Dogwood pattern. Shaped to create a springiness to better secure the napkins. 4" long x 3" wide x 4½" tall. Hallmark: 2A (Wendell August Forge). **$35.00**

Nut Bowl. Flower and leaf pattern. Serrated rim. Center holder accommodates nutcracker and six picks (picks absent in photo). 7" diameter x 4" tall. Hallmark: 24A (Wilson Metal). **$10.00**

Nut Bowl. Pattern of flowers, berries, and a butterfly. Looped wire handles. Holder for nutcracker and six picks. Serrated lip. 10" diameter x 5" tall. Unmarked. **$10.00**

Paperweight. Flying ducks pattern. 5" long x 3" wide. Hallmark: 2A (Wendell August Forge). **$75.00**

Note Book Cover. Tree pattern. 7" wide x 8" tall. Hallmark: 2F (Wendell August Forge). **$250.00**

Pitcher. Bamboo pattern. Ice lip on rolled edge. Beautiful detail on this piece. 5" diameter x 8" tall. Hallmark: 9C (Everlast). **$35.00**

Pitcher. Wild rose pattern. Small ice lip inside spout. Ear handle. 6" diameter x 8" tall. Hallmark: 5B (Continental). **$35.00**

Pitcher. Tulip pattern. Ice lip applied inside spout. Skinny ear-shaped handle. 5" diameter x 9" tall. Hallmark: 16B (Rodney Kent). **$45.00**

Pitcher. Chrysanthemum pattern. Applied leaf at bottom of handle. Ice lip applied inside spout. 6" diameter x 9" tall. Hallmark: 5A (Continental). **$45.00**

Pitcher. There are concentric bands around the entire pitcher. Large "C" handle. Small spout without ice lip. Copper anodized. In the early 1950s companies put out cottage cheese in colored anodized glasses which could be used for iced tea once the food product was eaten. Glasses came in turquoise, teal, red, chartreuse, yellow, magenta, and dark green, in addition to the copper. For a nominal amount, one could send for this pitcher to have a complete iced tea set. 6" diameter x 8" tall. Hallmark: 55 (Color Craft). **$5.00**

Pitcher. Acorn and leaf pattern. Ice lip applied inside spout. Aluminum wire coiled around handle. 6" diameter x 8" tall. Hallmark: 5C (Continental). **$25.00**

Pitcher. Hammered effect. Swedish modern style. Straight handle. 6" diameter x 7" tall. Unmarked. **$10.00**

Pitcher. Hammered effect. No ice lip. Scalloped edge. Small "D" shaped handle. 6" diameter x 8" tall. Unmarked. **$5.00**

Pitcher. Hammered effect. Small spout. No ice lip. Scalloped rim. Greek Key handle. 5" diameter x 7" tall. Hallmark: 44B (Nasco Italy). **$5.00**

Pitcher. Hammered effect. Ice lip applied over spout. Tall ear-shaped handle. 6" diameter x 8" tall. Hallmark: 9B (Everlast). **$5.00**

Pitcher. Hammered effect. 6" diameter x 8" tall. Hallmark: 3A (Buenilum). **$35.00**

Pitcher. Hammered effect. Flaring rim with rolled lip. Ice lip applied inside. Large rounded handle. 6" diameter x 8" tall. Hallmark: 13 (Gailstyn). **$5.00**

Pitcher. Hammered effect. Slightly flared top and bottom. Scroll handle. 5" diameter x 7" tall. Hallmark: 44A (Nasco Italy). **$5.00**

Syrup Pitcher. Hammered effect. Black plastic handle has thumb rest on attached lid. 4" diameter x 6" tall. Marked: Stratford-On-Avon. **$15.00**

Syrup Pitcher. Plain. Angled strap handle has thumb rest on attached lid. 3" diameter x 6" tall. Marked: Viko The Popular Aluminum. **$10.00**

Cigarette and Match Holders. Individual size holders for four cigarettes and a book of matches. Could also accommodate a place card and might have been intended for a formal dining table. Hammered effect. 3" long x 2½" tall. Hallmark: 45A (DePonceau). **$50.00** each

During the late 1940s and early 1950s, hobbyists became involved with metal working at home. Many fine example are still in circulation, although we also find many that lack artistic aptitude. While many were simply hammered or embossed, most employed the use of acids to etch the design onto the metal.

Hobbyist Plaque. Parrot on a branch. Fluted edge. Etched scalloped edge around main theme. 14" diameter. Unmarked. **$2.00**

Hobbyist Plaque. Flying duck and cat-tail. Fluted edge. Etched scalloped edge around main theme. 14" diameter. Unmarked. **$2.00**

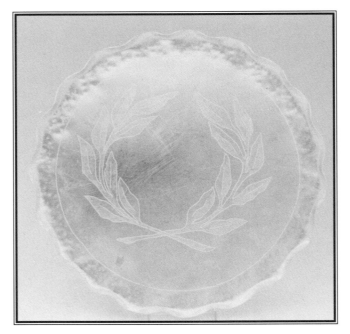

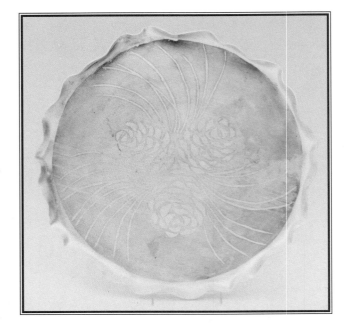

Hobbyist Plaque. Laurel wreach design is off-center. Hammered and fluted rim. 14" diameter. Unmarked. **$2.00**

Hobbyist Plaque. Pine cone design. Scalloped and fluted edge. 11" diameter. Unmarked. **$2.00**

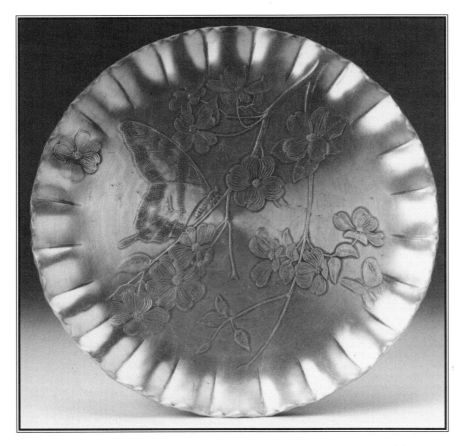

Plate. Dogwood and Butterfly. 10" diameter. Mark: 1A (Arthur Armour). **$45.00**

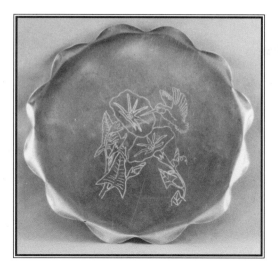

Hobbyist Plaque. Hummingbird and floral spray produced by machine engraving. Scalloped and fluted edge. 16" diameter. Unmarked. **$6.00**

Plate. Signing of the Declaration of Independence. 9" diameter. Artist signed: Natlae. Hallmark: 2D (Wendell August Forge). Marked: Handmade for Triangular Springs. **$45.00**

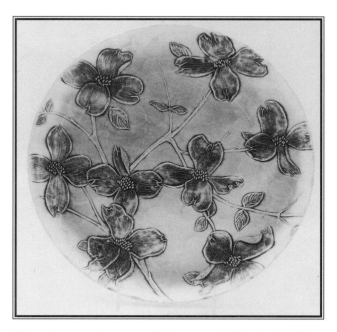

Plate. Dogwood pattern. 9" diameter. Hallmark: 2A (Wendell August Forge). **$35.00**

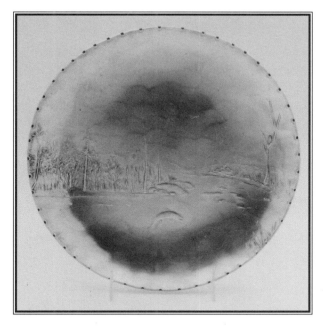

Plate. Scenic river and jumping trout. Crimped edge. 8½" diameter. Hallmark: 2B (Wendell August Forge). **$65.00**

Plate. Grove City college. 11" diameter. Hallmark: 45A (DePonceau). **$35.00**

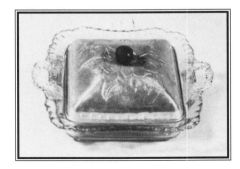

Dresser Dish. Single rose pattern. Black wood finial. Glass has bead effect on rim. Handles have leaf embossing. 5¾" wide (7" including handles) x 3" tall. Hallmark: 11 (Farberware). **$10.00**

Dresser Set. Two glass dishes with aluminum lids on aluminum stand. Classic Rodney Kent design with ribbon and flowers. Tray is 12" long (13¼" including feet) x 6" wide. Dishes are 4½" diameter x 1½" deep. Dish with cover is 3¼" tall. Hallmark: 16B (Rodney Kent). Marked: 403. **$45.00**

Purse. Chrysanthemum pattern. Embossed on hammered background. Moveable straps are hammered. 8" long x 5" wide x 5" tall, excluding the handles. Unmarked. **$250.00**

Popcorn Popper. Ducks. 9" diameter. Hallmark: 2B (Wendell August). **$75.00**

Saucepan. Flower band pattern on lid. Two quart size. Twisted wire handle. Acorn finial. 9" diameter. Unmarked. **$10.00**

Sherbets. Plain. Glass inserts in aluminum bases. Bases are anodized in magenta, red, chartreuse, turquoise, yellow, and light blue. These probably were also available in a dark green and copper as were the glasses and pitchers. Unmarked. **$15.00** all

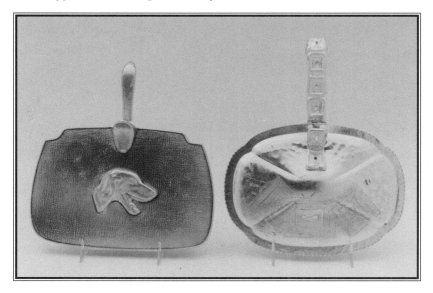

Silent Butlers. Left has dog's head pattern. 8" long x 5½" wide. Hallmark: 48 (Bruce Fox). Right has geometric pattern. 7" long x 5" wide. Unmarked. Left, **$35.00**; Right, **$5.00**

Silent Butlers. Left has wheat pattern. 6½" diameter. Hallmark: 18 (Kraftware). Right has rose pattern. 6" diameter. Hallmark: 9B (Everlast). **$10.00** each

Silent Butlers. Left has sunburst flower pattern. 6" diameter. Unmarked. Right has rose spray pattern. 6" diameter. Hallmark: 9C (Everlast). **$10.00** each

Silent Butlers. Left has berry pattern. 6" diameter. Hallmark: 9B (Everlast). Right has wild rose pattern. 6" diameter. Hallmark: 5B (Continental). Left, **$10.00**; Right, $**20.00**

Silent Butlers. Left has bamboo pattern. 6" diameter. Hallmark: 9C (Everlast). Right has bird sitting on a branch. Nice detail in pattern. Fluted and scalloped edge. Open wire handle. 6" diameter. Marked N.S.Co. Left, **$10.00**; Right, **$15.00**

Silent Butlers. Left has pine cone pattern. 7" diameter. Hallmark: 2A (Wendell August Forge). Right has grape cluster and fine fluted and scalloped edge. Open wire handle. 6" diameter. Unmarked. Left, **$15.00**; Right, **$10.00**

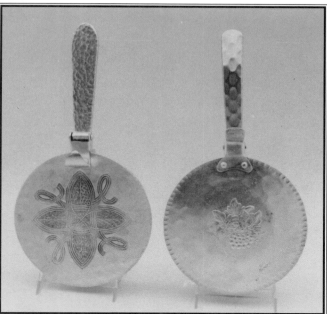

Silent Butlers Left has Celtic knot or curvilinear pattern. 6" diameter. Hallmark: 4A (Canterbury Arts). Right has grape cluster and leaf pattern. Crimped edge. 6" diameter. Hallmark: 9C (Everlast). Left, **$10.00**; Right, **$10.00**

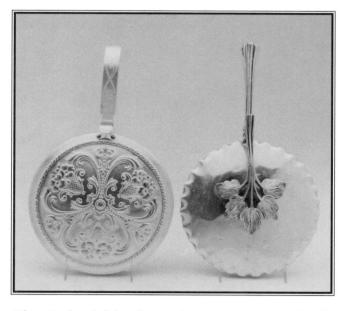

Silent Butler. Left has flowers in sconce pattern. High polish. 6" diameter. Unmarked. Right has leaf pattern. This is an unusual applied pattern with the stems of the leaf rising up to form the thumb hold on the lid. The handle is also leaf stem configuration. Fluted edge. 7" diameter. Unmarked. **$10.00** each

Silent Butlers. Left has wild roses pattern. 8" diameter. Hallmark: 5B (Continental). Right has tomato pattern. 6" diameter. Hallmark: 9B (Everlast). Left, **$15.00**; Right, **$10.00**

Silent Butlers. Right has acorn and leaf pattern. 7" diameter. Hallmark: 5C (Continental). Left has wild rose pattern. Open flower finial on lid. 7" diameter. Hallmark: 5B (Continental). **$25.00** each

Salad Set. 12" long. No mark. **$45.00**

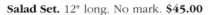

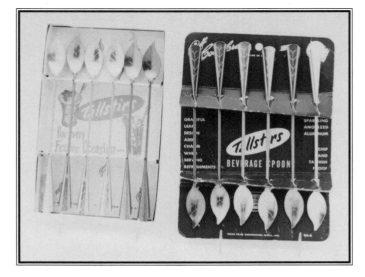

Tallstirs Beverage Spoons. Color anodized spoons with leaf shaped bowls and stem and leaf markings on handles. Although there is no hallmark on the metal, the card to the right is clearly marked Color Craft Corporation, Indianapolis, Indiana. **$30.00** each set

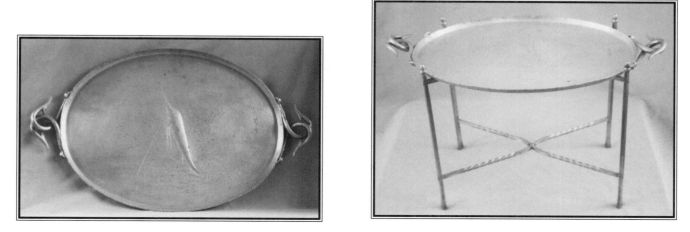

Table (close up of tray). Twisted wrought x-braces attached to hammered legs with acorn finial retainers. Tray has a jumping marlin design. Handles are beautifully unique entwined fishhooks. A very striking tray. 28" long x 17" wide x 19" tall. Hallmark: 2B (Wendell August Forge). **$500.00**

Table. Twisted cable x-brace attached to twisted cable legs with stanchion finial. Tray has a pine cone and needles pattern. Twisted cable handle encircles the tray, being attached at four points. 21" diameter x 19" tall. Hallmark: 2B (Wendell August Forge). **$450.00**

Tureen and Ladle. 8" x 13". Ladle 14" long. Hallmark: Cellini-Craft, Argental. Tureen, **$175.00**; Ladle, **$45.00**

Bar Tray. Flying ducks and cat-tail pattern. 16" long x 9" wide. Unmarked. **$30.00**

Bar Tray. Anchor, rope, and seagulls pattern. Applied handles. 15" long x 9" wide. Hallmark: 9B (Everlast). **$30.00**

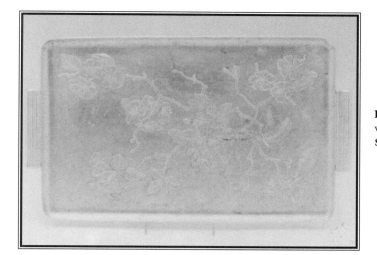

Bar Tray. Wild rose pattern. 15" long x 9" wide. Hallmark: 2A (Wendell August Forge). **$40.00**

Bar Tray. Pine cone pattern. No handles. 20" long x 8" wide. Hallmark: 9C (Everlast). **$10.00**

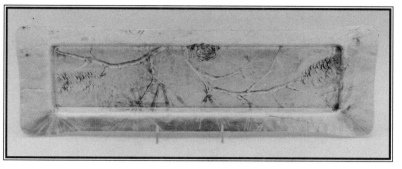

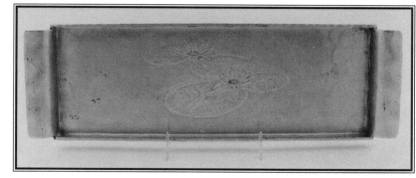

Bar Tray. Water lily pattern. Self-handled. 17" long x 8" wide. Hallmark: 1A (Arthur Armour). **$45.00**

Bar Tray. Flying geese scenic pattern. Self-handled. 17" long x 9" wide. Hallmark: 2B (Wendell August Forge). **$50.00**

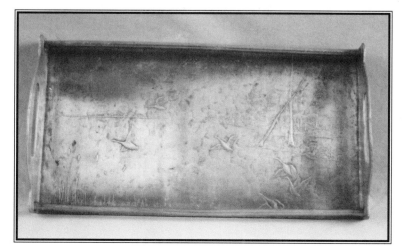

Bar Tray. Bird dog with split rail fence scenic pattern. Self-handled. 17" long x 9" wide. Hallmark: 2B (Wendell August Forge). **$90.00**

Bread Tray. Hammered effect. Loop handles with tulip finial. Note 50 cent price tag. Was this a steal, or what? Hallmark: 3B (Buenilum). **$15.00**

Beverage Tray. All-over vine and flower pattern. Applied handles. 14" long x 10" wide x 3" tall Hallmark: 17A (Keystone Ware). **$10.00**

Beverage Tray. All-over vine and flower pattern. Applied handles. 7" long x 8" wide x 4" tall. Hallmark: 17A (Keystone Ware). **$10.00**

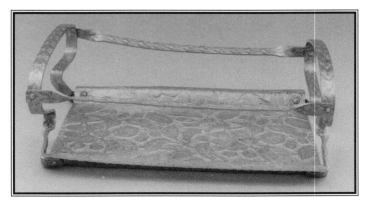

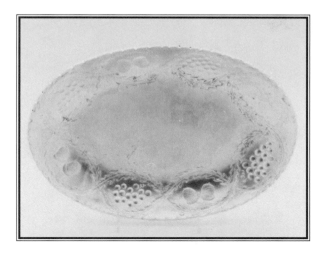

Bread Tray. Acorns and grapes in floral chain pattern. 11" long x 7" wide. Hallmark: 2C (Wendell August Forge). **$45.00**

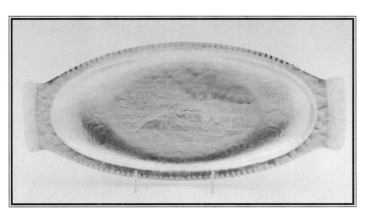

Bread Tray. Wild rose pattern. 13" long x 6" wide. Hallmark: 5B (Continental). **$15.00**

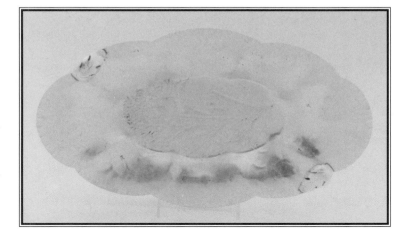

Bread Tray. Chrysanthemum pattern. Two applied leaves to scalloped edge. 11" long x 8" wide. Hallmark: 5C (Continental). **$25.00**

Bread Tray. Scroll pattern in center. Roses in urns around edge. Decorated edges down sides. 13" long x 7" wide. Unmarked. **$5.00**

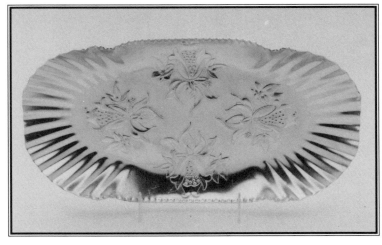

Bread Tray. Stylized flower pattern. 11" long x 6" wide. **$5.00**

Close up of stylized flower pattern.

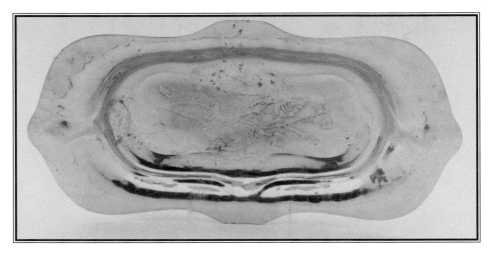

Bread Tray. Berry vine pattern. 13" long x 7" wide. Unmarked. **$5.00**

Bread Trays. Left is heavy grape pattern. 12" long x 6" wide. Unmarked. Right is narcissus pattern. 12" long x 7" wide. Unmarked. **$5.00** each

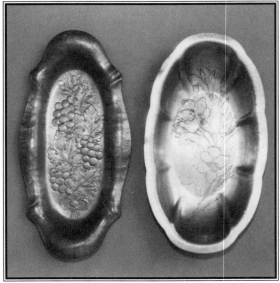

Bread Tray. Orchid pattern. Scalloped edge. 12" long x 6" wide. Unmarked. **$5.00**

Bread Tray. Chrysanthemum pattern. Scroll edge. 12" long x 7" wide. Hallmark: 28 (Forman). **$5.00**

Bread Tray. Apple blossom pattern. Fluted sides. 13" long x 9" wide. Unmarked. **$5.00**

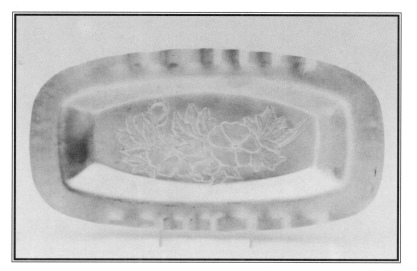

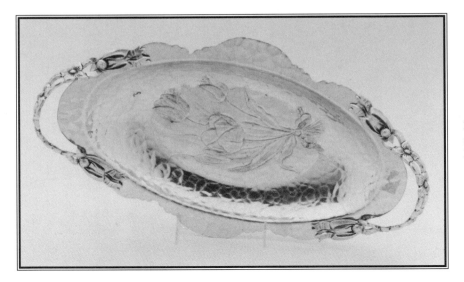

Bread Tray. Tulip pattern. Applied flower and ribbon handles. 13" long x 8" wide. Hallmark: 16 B (Rodney Kent). **$25.00**

Bread Tray. Floral spray pattern. 12" long x 7" wide. Unmarked. **$5.00**

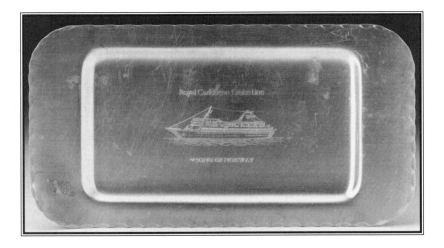

Bread Tray. Royal Caribbean Cruise Lines. 12" x 7". No mark. **$5.00**

Bread Tray. Deer. 13" x 7". Mark: Hand wrought by L. Gene Stewart; also, paper label on back "Creations in wood, metal, and plaster by Rev. L. Gene Stewart, etc." **$35.00**

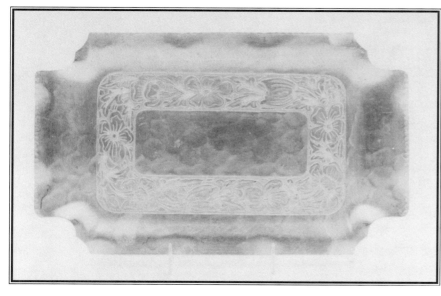

Bread Tray. Flower band pattern. Self-handled. 12" long x 7" wide. Hallmark: 9A (Everlast). **$5.00**

Cheese and Cracker Tray. All-over flower and vine pattern. 20" diameter. Hallmark: 33 (Handwrought). **$5.00**

Cheese and Cracker Tray. Acorn and leaf pattern. 15" diameter. Hallmark: 5C (Continental). **$15.00**

Relish Tray. Flying geese pattern repeated in each of four compartments. Self-handled. 16" long x 5" wide. Hallmark: 1A (Arthur Armour). **$75.00**

Relish Tray. Italian Majolica inserts. 17" diameter. Mark: Cellini-Craft, Argental. **$265.00**

Relish Tray. 17" diameter. Marked: Cellini-Craft, Argental. **$165.00**

Sandwich Tray. Crested crane and bamboo pattern. Applied handles. 9" diameter. Hallmark: 15 (Hand Forged). **$35.00**

Sandwich Trays. Left is the poppy pattern. 10" diameter. Hallmark: 2A (Wendell August Forge). Right is the pine cone pattern. 12" diameter. Marked: Hammercraft. Made in Canada. Left, **$45.00**; Right, **$10.00**

Sandwich Tray. Tennis player. 10" x 16". Hallmark: Hyman Blum, Pittsburgh, PA, U.S.A. **$45.00**

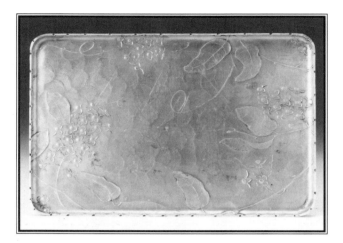

Sandwich Tray. Bittersweet. 8" x 11". Hallmark: 2A (Wendell August). **$35.00**

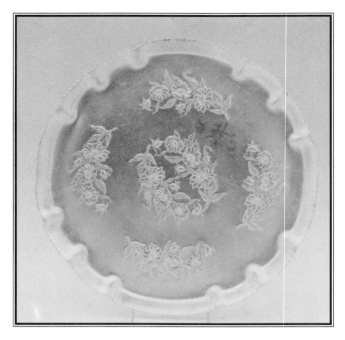

Sandwich Tray. Flower spray pattern. Fluted and serrated edge. 12" diameter. Hallmark: 35 (Embossed Aluminum). **$5.00**

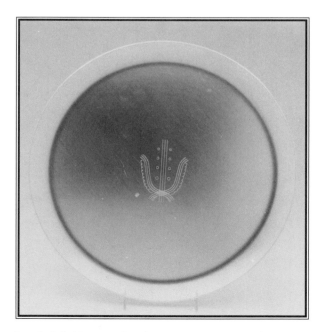

Sandwich Tray. Stylized cactus pattern. 12" diameter. Hallmark: 30 (Kensington). **$15.00**

Sandwich Tray. Dogwood pattern. Fluted edge. 10" diameter. Hallmark: 8 stamped over hallmark 38 (Admiration). **$5.00**

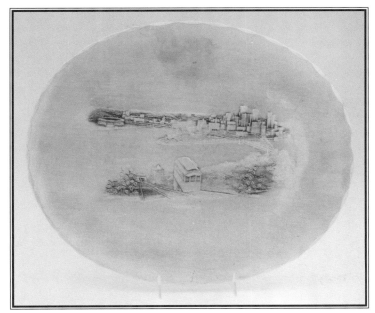

Sandwich Tray. Pittsburgh skyline pattern with railway car. 13" long x 11" wide. Hallmark: 2C (Wendell August Forge). **$65.00**

Sandwich Tray. Acorn and leaf pattern. Applied handles. Fluted edge. 11" diameter. Unmarked. **$25.00**

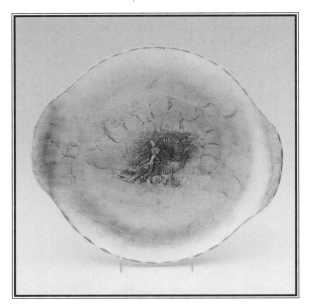

Sandwich Tray. Grouse pattern. Self-handled. 10" diameter. Hallmark: 2E (Wendell August Forge). Marked: Handmade for the Annual Mid-Atlantic Skeet Championship. **$65.00**

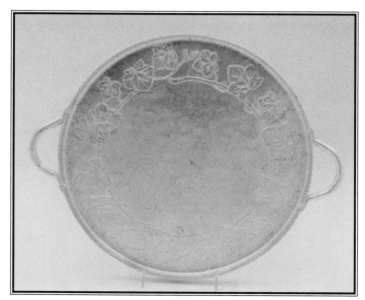

Sandwich Tray. Ivy vine pattern. Applied handles. 11" diameter. Hallmark: 9B (Everlast). **$5.00**

Sandwich Tray. Four flying duck pattern. 12" long x 10" wide. Hallmark: 9B (Everlast). **$15.00**

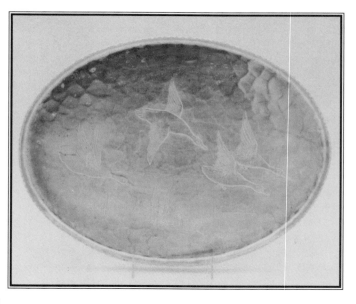

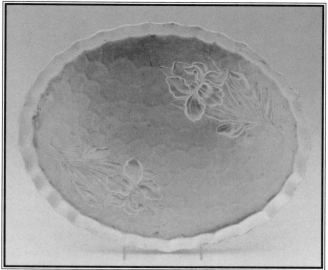

Sandwich Tray. Iris pattern. Fluted edge. 12" long x 10" wide. Unmarked. **$5.00**

Sandwich Tray. Fruit and flower pattern. Serrated rim. 13" diameter. Hallmark: 29 (Hand Finished). **$5.00**

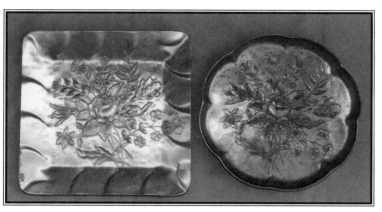

Sandwich Trays. Left is the rose spray pattern. 12" square. Hallmark: 9C (Everlast). Right is also a rose spray pattern. Scalloped, serrated edge. 11" diameter. Hallmark: 9C (Everlast). **$5.00** each

Sandwich Tray. Two birddogs pattern. Of special interest to sportsmen is that one is a pointer and the other a setter. Fluted edge. 12" square. Hallmark: 37 (Lehman). **$35.00**

Sandwich Tray or Child's Dinner Tray. Miscellaneous decorations of alphabet, numbers, animals, toys, and several words. 14" long x 8" wide. Hallmark: 2A (Wendell August Forge). **$200.00**

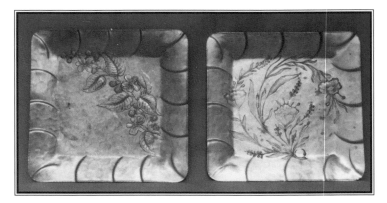

Sandwich Trays. One flower spray pattern and one berry and leaf pattern. 13" square. Unmarked. **$5.00** each

Sandwich Trays. Top is the scenic pine pattern. Applied handles. 13" long x 9" wide. Hallmark: 1A (Arthur Armour). Bottom is a sailing regatta scene pattern. 14" long x 9" wide. Hallmark: 2B (Wendell August Forge). Top, **$40.00**; Bottom, **$50.00**

Sandwich Trays. Top is the lily pad or lotus pattern. Applied handles. 15" long x 10" wide. Hallmark: 1B (ArthuArmour). Bottom has three pattern panels, one vegetables, one fish and lobster, and one fruits. 16" long x 11" wide. Hallmark: 17D (Keystone Ware). Top, **$60.00**; Bottom, **$10.00**

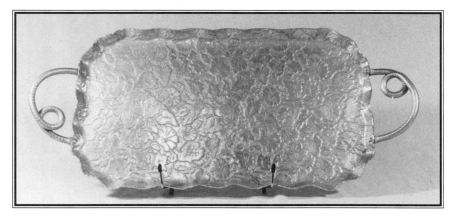

Serving Tray. All-over flower and vine pattern. Full loop handle at each end. 18" long (22¾ with handle) x 10½" wide. Hallmark: 10A (Farber & Shlevin). Marked: 1486. **$5.00**

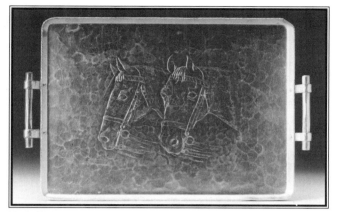

Serving Tray. Horses. 12" x 16". Hallmark: 9B (Everlast). **$35.00**

Serving Tray. Knightly-Friends, 1940, 35th Anniversary. 17" diameter. Hallmark: 17C (Keystone). **$15.00**

Serving Tray. Deer and Geese. 12" x 16". Hallmark: 5A (Continental). **$75.00**

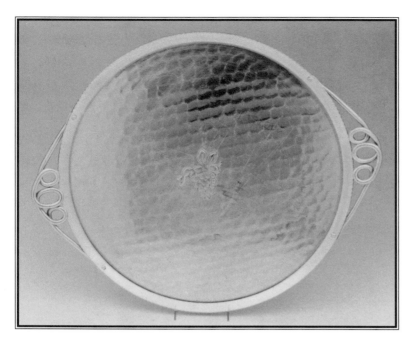

Serving Tray. Grape cluster pattern. Wire loop handles with three loops on each side. 17" diameter. Unmarked. **$5.00**

Serving Tray. Flower spray pattern. Applied handles with leaf and stem motif. 14" diameter. Hallmark: 14A (Hammercraft). **$5.00**

Serving Tray. Leaping gazelle pattern. 15" diameter. 9 Unmarked. **$5.00**

Serving Tray. Fruit pattern. Applied handles are a rod held by a coil of wire. 17" diameter. Hallmark: 15 (Hand Forged). **$5.00**

Serving Tray. Floral pattern. Scalloped, fluted, and serrated edge. 14" diameter. Hallmark: 24A (Wilson Metal). **$5.00**

Serving Tray. Pheasant pattern. 18" diameter. Marked: Westbend. **$5.00**

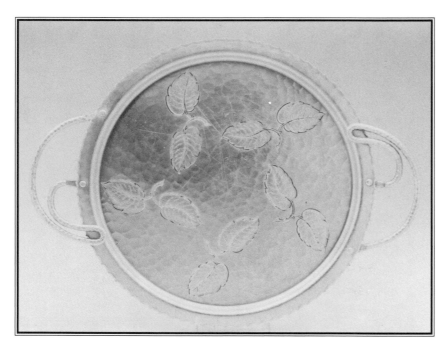

Serving Tray. Leaf pattern. Folded wire handles. 16" diameter. Hallmark: 11 (Farberware). **$5.00**

Serving Tray. Rose pattern. Applied handles with leaves. 17" diameter. Hallmark: 5C (Continental). **$10.00**

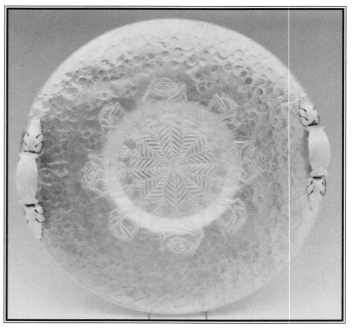

Serving Tray. Floral pattern. 15" diameter. Hallmark: 12B (Federal Silver). **$5.00**

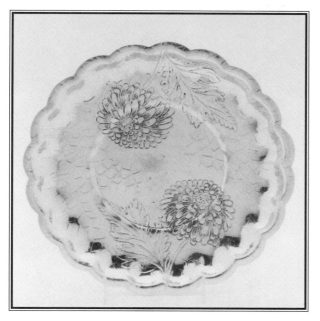

Serving Tray. Chrysanthemum pattern. Scalloped edge. 14" diameter. Unmarked. **$5.00**

Serving Tray. Duck hunter, bird dog, and ducks scenic pattern. 18" diameter. Hallmark: 58 (LA Hand Forged). **$95.00**

Serving Tray. Fisherman and fish scenic pattern. 18" diameter. Hallmark: 15 (Hand Forged). **$85.00**

Serving Tray. Berry and leaf pattern. China insert with two Victorian ladies. China marked Faberware Brooklyn New York. 16" diameter. Hallmark: 6 (Cromwell). **$55.00**

Serving Tray. Spun aluminum with blue stylized flower ceramic lining in bottom (not an insert). 11⅛" diameter x 1½" deep. Hallmark: 3C (Buenilum). **$65.00**

Serving Tray. Morning glory pattern. China insert has fruit and flower compote. China marked Made in U.S.A. Limoges. 11" diameter. Hallmark: 6 (Cromwell). **$55.00**

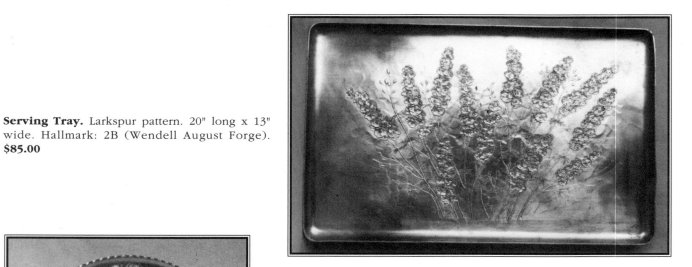

Serving Tray. Larkspur pattern. 20" long x 13" wide. Hallmark: 2B (Wendell August Forge). **$85.00**

Serving Tray. Hibiscus pattern. Ceramic insert with compote, fruit and flower design. Insert marked "Limoges," "Imperial Victorian Pattern," and "Made for Farberware." 11¾" diameter. Hallmark: 11 (Farberware). **$55.00**

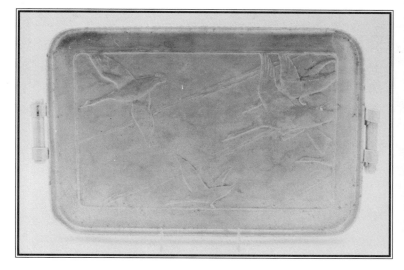

Serving Tray. Flying geese pattern. Applied handles. 13" long x 9" wide. Hallmark: 1B (Arthur Armour). **$85.00**

Serving Trays. Left is a rectangular tray with the grape clusters and vine pattern, with a pattern sequence at each end. Applied handles. Square corners. 18" long x 10" wide. Hallmark: 9C (Everlast). Right is an oblong tray with a hammered effect background with double rose spray at each end by the handle. Applied wire loop handles. Rounded corners. 10" long x 8" wide. Unmarked. Left, **$10.00**; Right, **$5.00**

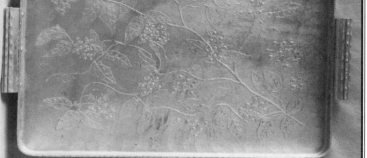

Serving Tray. Bittersweet pattern. Applied handles. 21" long x 12" wide. Unmarked. **$30.00**

Serving Tray. Highly polished. Handles are decorated with fox hunting scenes. 23" long x 14" wide. Hallmark: 30 (Kensington). **$35.00**

Serving Tray. Fox hunting scene pattern. Applied handles. 17" long x 12" wide. Unmarked. **$45.00**

Serving Tray. Fox hunting scene pattern. Self-handled. 20" long x 14" wide. Hallmark: 5C (Continental). **$65.00**

Serving Tray. Horse head in horseshoe pattern. The word "WESTS" is incorporated into the horseshoe. 15" long x 9" wide. Hallmark: 2C (Wendell August Forge). **$65.00**

Serving Tray. Sailboat pattern. 16" long x 12" wide. Hallmark: 9B (Everlast). **$20.00**

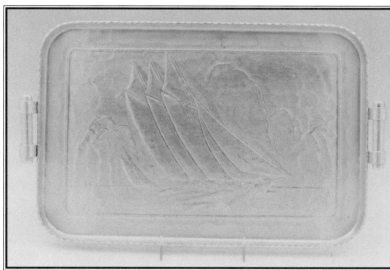

Serving Tray. Sailing ship pattern. Applied handles. 13" long x 9" wide. Hallmark: (Arthur Armour) **$65.00**

Serving Tray. Sailing ship pattern. Applied handles. 18" long x 11" wide. Hallmark: 9B (Everlast). **$25.00**

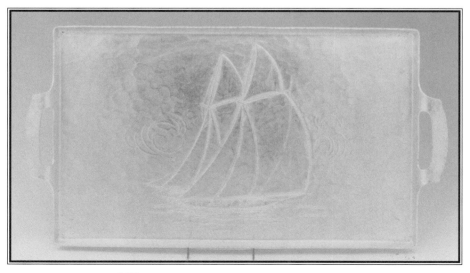

Serving Tray. Intricate scenic design with windmill, house, boat, and mountain. Wire loop handles with leaf finials applied. Crimped edge. 18" long x 13" wide. Hallmark: 6 (Cromwell). **$35.00**

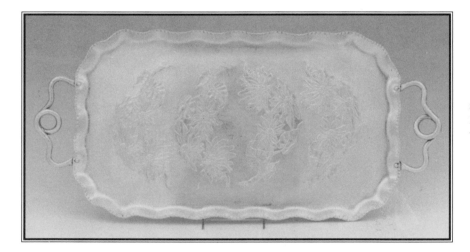

Serving Tray. Poinsettia pattern. Wire loop handles applied. 18" long x 11" wide. Unmarked. **$5.00**

Serving Tray. Fruit band pattern. Wire loop handles applied. Oblong shape. 19" long x 13" wide. Hallmark: 6 (Cromwell). **$5.00**

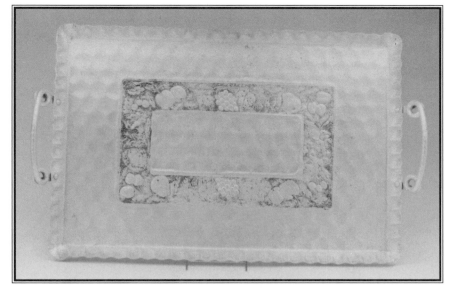

Serving Tray. Fruit band pattern. Wire loop handles applied. Square corners. 18" long x 12" wide. Hallmark: 6 (Cromwell). **$5.00**

Serving Tray. Apple blossom pattern. 16" long x 10" wide. Hallmark: 9A (Everlast). **$5.00**

Serving Tray. Goldfish pattern. Walnut handles applied. Beading around pattern panel. 14" long x 10" wide. Unmarked. **$45.00**

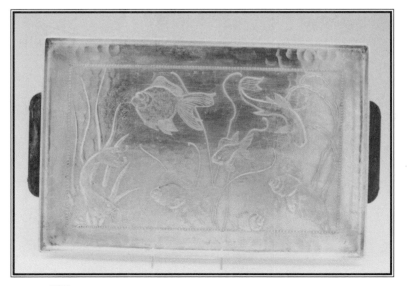

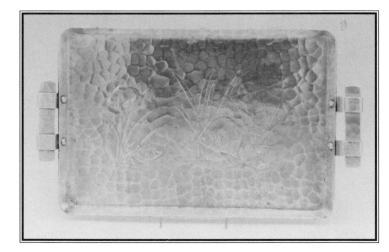

Serving Tray. Tropical fish pattern. Applied handle. 15" long x 10" wide. Hallmark: 22 (World Hand Forged). **$35.00**

Serving Tray. Acorn and leaf pattern. Applied leaf handles. 20" long x 14" wide. Hallmark: 5C (Continental). **$20.00**

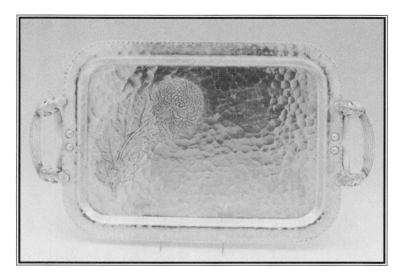

Serving Tray. Chrysanthemum pattern. Applied handles with leaves. Hammered background. 11" long x 8" wide. Hallmark: 5A (Continental). **$30.00**

Serving Tray. Rose spray pattern. Large applied handle. 16" long x 10" wide. Unmarked. **$5.00**

Serving Tray. Tulip pattern. Applied flower and ribbon handle. 20" long x 14" wide. Hallmark: 16B (Rodney Kent). **$35.00**

Serving Tray. Bamboo pattern. Applied bamboo handles. 16" long x 12" wide. Hallmark: 9C (Everlast). **$15.00**

Serving Tray. Bamboo pattern. Applied bamboo handles. 14" long x 9" wide. Hallmark: 9C (Everlast). **$25.00**

Serving Tray. Intaglio flying duck scenic pattern. 15" long x 9" wide. Unmarked. **$5.00**

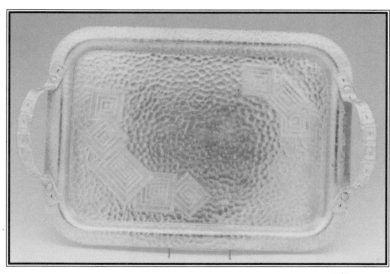

Serving Tray. Geometric design pattern. Applied handle. 16" long x 12" wide. Unmarked. **$5.00**

Serving Tray. Coach and four horses. 10" x 13". Hallmark: Clayton Sheasle (?). **$125.00**

Serving Tray. Rose pattern. Applied rose embossed handle. 18" long x 13" wide Hallmark: 5A (Continental). **$10.00**

Serving Tray. Rose pattern. Applied leaf motif handle. Clipped corners give hexagon shape to tray. Same as 648 except for handles and shape. 18" long x 13" wide. Hallmark: 5A (Continental). **$10.00**

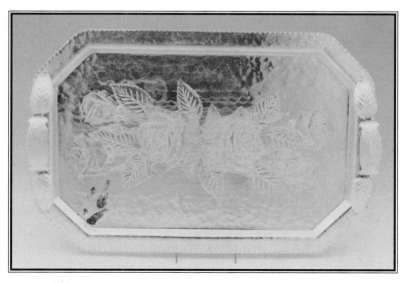

Snack Tray. Sail boat. 5" x 8". Hallmark: 2C (Wendell August). **$45.00**

Snack Tray. Flying quail scenic pattern. Good detail. Scalloped edge. 9" long x 7" wide. Hallmark: 2C (Wendell August Forge). Marked: Handmade for S. A. Wagner. **$60.00**

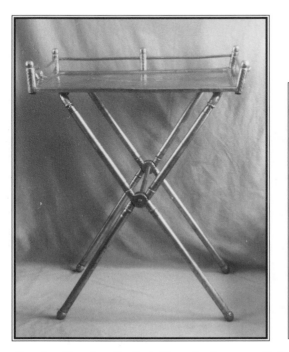

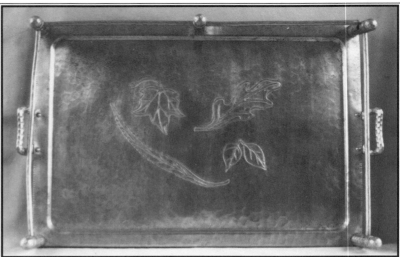

Serving Stand or Butler's Tray. Leaf pattern. X-shaped frame with center support rod. Tray has applied railing on three sides. 25" long x 18" wide x 34" tall. Hallmark: 9F (Everlast). **$225.00**

Snack Tray. Leaping trout scenic pattern. Hammered background. 9" long x 6" wide. Hallmark. 2A (Wendell August Forge). Marked: Quaker State Motor Oil. **$60.00**

Snack Tray. Fisherman netting a fish pattern. Stamped floral design around edge. Marked "Norge" on front. 7" square. Unmarked. **$6.00**

Snack Tray. Flying ducks and cat-tails pattern. Lipped. Self-handled. 6" long x 4" wide. Unmarked. **$3.00**

Snack Tray. Norge (Norway). 7" square. No mark. **$3.00**

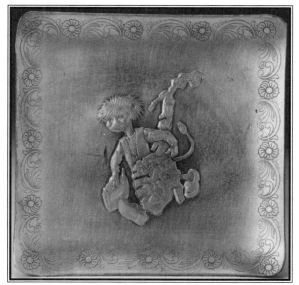

Snack Trays. Left is a fruit pattern. Right is a heron scenic pattern. Lipped. Self-handled. 10" long x 6" wide. Fruit Unmarked. Heron Hallmark: 38 (Admiration). Left, **$2.00**; Right, **$3.00**

Snack Trays. Each has only one handle. Left is a flower spray pattern. 6" long x 4" wide. Unmarked. Right is wild rose pattern. 6" long x 4" wide. Unmarked. **$1.00** each

Snack Trays. Left a flying geese pattern. Lipped. Self-handled. 7" long x 3" wide. Hallmark: 1A (Arthur Armour); Middle pattern is shocks of wheat in a field. 6" long x 4" wide. Hallmark: 2A (Wendell August Forge); On the back "Toastmasters" has been added; Right is the angel fish pattern. Lipped. 6" long x 3" wide. Hallmark: 1B (Arthur Armour). Left, **$25.00**; Middle, **$20.00**; Right, **$25.00**

Snack Set. Flying duck pattern. Serving tray and two snack trays. Self handled. Serrated edge on lip. Serving tray is 12" long x 9" wide. Snack trays are 6" long x 4" wide. Unmarked. Serving tray, **$10.00**; Snack tray, **$3.00** each

Snack Tray and Coaster. Heraldic shield pattern with a knight's helmet, three birds, and a hand. Tray is 6" long x 4" wide. Coaster is 3" diameter. Hallmark. Tray, **$30.00**; Coaster, **$15.00** 2E (Wendell August Forge)

Snack Tray. Amish scene. 5" x 10". Hallmark: 2C (Wendell August). **$65.00**

Tidbit Tray. Pressed panels of fruit and flowers. Four compartments. Center handle has loop finial. 9" square. Hallmark: 6 (Cromwell). **$5.00**

Snack Tray. Pheasant. 6" square. Hallmark: Silver Spring Forge, New Kingston, PA. Hand Crafted. **$35.00**

Snack Tray Set. Turkey, Ducks, Dogwood, and Pine. 5" square. Hallmark: 2B (Wendell August). **$45.00**

Tidbit Tray. Grape cable pattern. Fluted edge. Large loop handle in center. 6" diameter. Hallmark: 8 (Designed Aluminum). **$5.00**

Tidbit Tray. Dogwood pattern. Large loop handle in center. Fluted and scalloped edge. 6" diameter. Hallmark: 8 (Designed Aluminum). **$5.00**

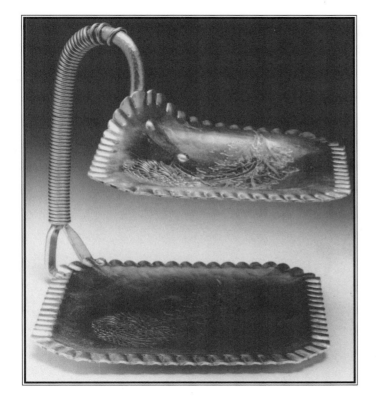

Tiered Tray. Chrysanthemum. 10" tall. Hallmark: 5C (Continental). **$45.00**

Tiered Tray. Ducks. 12" tall. Hallmark: 9B (Everlast). **$35.00**

Tiered Tray. Combination dogwood and pine cone pattern. Three tiers. Finial contains a white marble. 13" diameter x 12" tall. Unmarked. **$5.00**

Tiered Tray. Bamboo pattern. Two tiers. Bamboo finial. 10" diameter x 9" tall. Hallmark: 9C (Everlast). **$10.00**

Tiered Tray. Grapevine pattern. Two tiers. Large round finial. 10" diameter x 11" tall. Hallmark: 9C (Everlast). **$5.00**

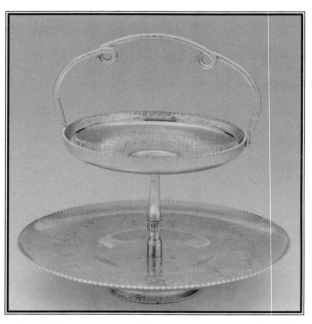

Tiered Tray. Fruit and flower pattern. Footed with a bail type handle with two inner loops. 14" diameter x 14" tall. Unmarked. **$5.00**

Tiered Tray. Tomato pattern. Two tiers. T-shaped handle. 11" diameter x 10" tall. Unmarked. **$5.00**

Tiered Tray. Rose pattern. Three tiers. Fluted. Handle lacks finial. 10" diameter x 11" tall. Unmarked. **$5.00**

Tiered Tray. Palm pattern. Fluted, scalloped, and serrated edges. Ornate round finial. 12" diameter x 9" tall. Unmarked. **$5.00**

Trivet. Acorn pattern. Extremely well defined pattern. Serrated edge. 10" diameter. Hallmark: 5C (Continental). **$10.00**

Trivets. Grapevine pattern. Larger is 10" diameter. Smaller is 7" long x 5½" wide. Hallmark: 9C (Everlast). Large, **$10.00**; Small, **$5.00**

Trivet. Pine cone pattern. 11" long x 8" wide. Hallmark: 9C (Everlast). **$5.00**

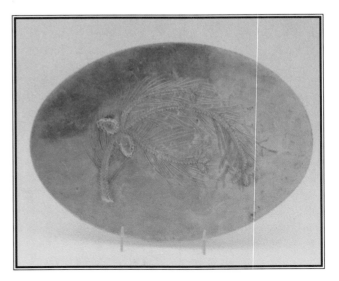

Trophy. Cocker Spaniel head in cast aluminum in an aluminum frame. 10" wide x 11" tall. Unmarked. **$45.00**

Tumblers. Anodized colors. Various hallmarks including: 54 (Zephyr Ware), 46 (Sunburst), 47 (Bascal), Italy and Japan. **$1.00** each

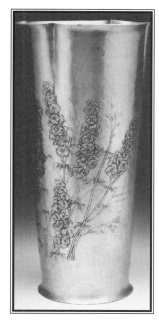

Vase, large or Umbrella Stand. Larkspur. 22" tall. Hallmark: 2B (Wendell August). **$285.00**

Vase. Chrysanthemum pattern. 5" diameter x 10" tall. Hallmark: 5C (Continental). **$85.00**

Wastebasket. Pine cone pattern. Scalloped and fluted rim. 11" diameter x 11" tall. Hallmark: 2A (Wendell August Forge). **$150.00**

WHIMSIES

If you love aluminum but don't have the space to store or display it, don't give up hope. Look for the items you can display in the room you have, or specialize, like collecting coasters or other small items. Some collectors indulge their love for aluminum by seeking out "whimsies." Now, *whimsey* is a term you will find in many collectible areas where there are handcrafted items. End-of-the-day blown glass items with a myriad of colors or end-of-the-cane marbles could be called whimsies. Whimsies are also the little items artisans made out of scraps to take home for their children. But don't let the term fool you. Whimsies can also be the legitimate collectible item in a smaller version, or it can be the odd little pieces, not your run-of-the-mill items, that you cannot categorize anywhere else. Those lovers of aluminum who do not have the room to store and display it, can still indulge their "whim" to collect aluminum with "whimsies."

The aluminum items which make up the bulk of this book were produced from the 1930s to the 1960s with a few new pieces which are being imported from Italy and probably Japan. But it was the Victorian Age when aluminum finally came down to 50-odd cents a pound, and many household items began sprouting up in aluminum or with aluminum trims. The cigar holder in this section has engraving on it which any jewelry collector can tell you is right out of the 1890s. The inhaler and the flashlight date from the time between tin or steel and plastic, when a light-weight substance was needed for a throw-away item. Even if you really love the large decorative items, have the space to store it and decorate with it when you can, don't overlook the whimsies. They are fun to seek and a joy to find!

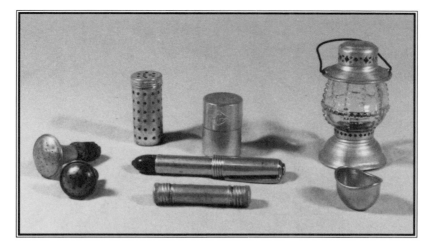

Nozzles, Herb Infuser, Film Canister, Eyewash Cup, Flashlight, and Inhaler. Left to right around the edge. Two nozzles which were poked into soft drink bottles and were used to sprinkle clothes in preparation of ironing. (Remember ironing clothes?) These items are 1½" long; and 2¼" long; The Herb Infuser has a screw-off top. It is 2½" long; The Film Canister is marked with the Agfa logo and "Made by Agfa Ansco Corporation in Binghampton, N.Y.;" A Candy Container shaped like kerosene lantern. Aluminum top and base with bail. Top screws off. 4" tall (5⅝" including handle); The Eyewash Cup is 1" tall, opening is 1½" x 1⅛"; Center: Flashlight has pocket clip, red tip. Holds AA batteries. 4½" long. Marked: Made in U.S.A. on cap end; Front: Anon-refillable Inhaler. Both ends screw off. One end is cone shaped inhaler; other is flat, similar to a sprinkler. 2¾" long. Unmarked. Nozzles, **$1.00** each; Infuser, **$8.00**; Film Canister, **$4.00**; Candy Container, **$22.00**; Eyewash Cup, **$5.00**; Flashlight, **$8.00**; Inhaler, **$6.00**

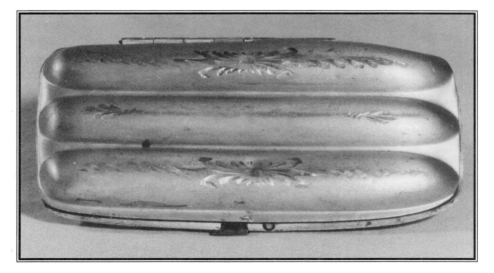

Cigar Holder. Hinged and locking. Shaped for three cigars. Floral engraving on top. 5⅛" long x 2⅝" wide. Unmarked. **$25.00**

Soap Dish. "Soap" in script on top. 3⅝" long x 2¾" wide x 1½" deep. Unmarked. **$5.00**

Upholstery Brush. Embossed "Renuzit's Eraser for Upholstered Furniture. Just dip in pan of Renuzit and erase the soil." Eraser part is hard felt-like material, similar to blackboard eraser. 4½" long x 2⅜" wide x 1" deep. Unmarked. **$10.00**

Cigarette Case. Two pieces slip together. 3½" collapsed expands to 3⅞" holder. 1½" x 1". **$5.00**

Spoon. "Short'ning and Ice Cream Spoon." Gold anodized. 8" long. Unmarked. **$2.00**

Fishing Reel. Marked "Lord Weldon." 3½" tall. Unmarked. **$28.00**

Dresser Container. Embossed "Kremola Makes the Skin Beautiful. Price $1.25. Dr. C. H. Berry Company, Chicago, New York." 2½" diameter x 1¼" deep. Unmarked. **$12.00**

Odds and Ends. Left is a bookend. "End of the Trail" design of Indian and horse. Cast. 5½" tall. Rear is a hood ornament or flag pole finial. Art Deco style Winged Victory holding laurel wreath. 6¾" tall. Right is a duck mail box ornament. Good detail. 4¼" tall x 4" wide. Front is a bridle bit. Engraved end pieces. 5¾" x 6½". Bookend, **$8.00** each, **$25.00** pair; Art Deco Piece, **$12.00**; Mail Box Ornament, **$10.00**; Bridle Bit, **$8.00**

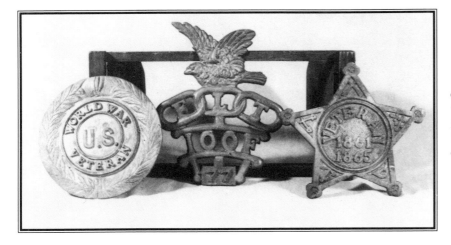

Cemetery Markers. Left is a laurel wreath. "World War Veteran U.S." in center. Middle is Odd Fellows logo. Right is a star. "Veteran 1861 – 1865" All cast. Unmarked. **$30.00** each

Vase. Petal-like panels on each of four sides. 5" tall x 6½" wide. Marked: "Country Ware copyright 1975" "Copyright Wilton, Columbia, PA, USA" and "700." Also has three indistinguishable marks in borders. **$10.00**

Ashtrays. Left is Jack in the Box, and right is Burger King. Both anodized gold. Jack in the Box is heavy foil composition, clearly a throw-away item. Burger King is regular aluminum item similar to coasters. Both 3½" diameter. Unmarked. **$1.00** each

Salt and Pepper Shakers. Weighted bottoms. Engraved with star and strip shield and "New York." 2½" tall. Unmarked. **$15.00**

ENDNOTES

1. LaVoisier quoted through Philip Farin, Gary B. Reibsamen and the *Metals Week* editorial staff, "Aluminum: Profile of an Industry" (New York: McGraw-Hill, 1969), p. 14.

2. Smith, George David, *From Monopoly to Competition: The Transformation of Alcoa 1888 – 1986*, (Cambridge [Eng.] : Cambridge University Press, 1986), p. 12.

3. Edwards, Junius, Francis C. Frary, Zag Jeffries, *Aluminum and Its Production* (New York: McGraw-Hill, 1930), p. 1 – 15.

4. Edwards, p. 1 – 15.

5. Carr, Charles C., *Alcoa, an American Enterprise* (New York, Toronto: Rinehart & Co., Inc. 1952), p. 24.

6. Smith, p. 16.

7. Edwards, p. 1 – 15.

8. Smith, quoting Fickes, Edwin S., "History of the Growth and Development of the Aluminum Company of America…," a typescript bound in Vol. 17 of *Histories of the Manufacturing Properties of the Aluminum Company of America …* (Alcoa Archives), p. 62.

9. Smith, p. 17.

10. Anderson, Robert, *The Metallurgy of Aluminum and Aluminum Alloys* (New York: Henry Carey Baird & Co., Inc., 1925), p. 279 – 280.

11. Carr, p. 111 – 115.

12. Edwards, p. 27.

13. Anderson, p. 141.

14. Carr, p. 120 – 124.

15. Engle, Nathanael, Homer Gregory, Robert Morse, *Aluminum* (Seattle: University of Washington, 1944), p. 325.

16. Anderson, p. 858 – 861.

COLLECTOR BOOKS

I n f o r m i n g   T o d a y ' s   C o l l e c t o r

For over two decades we have been keeping collectors informed on trends and values in all fields of antiques and collectibles.

DOLLS, FIGURES & TEDDY BEARS

4631	**Barbie Doll** Boom, 1986–1995, Augustyniak	$18.95
2079	**Barbie Doll** Fashion, Volume I, Eames	$24.95
4846	**Barbie Doll** Fashion, Volume II, Eames	$24.95
3957	**Barbie** Exclusives, Rana	$18.95
4632	**Barbie** Exclusives, Book II, Rana	$18.95
6022	The **Barbie Doll** Years, 5th Ed., Olds	$19.95
3810	**Chatty Cathy** Dolls, Lewis	$15.95
5352	Collector's Ency. of **Barbie** Doll Exclusives & More, 2nd Ed.,Augustyniak	$24.95
2211	Collector's Encyclopedia of **Madame Alexander** Dolls, Smith	$24.95
4863	Collector's Encyclopedia of **Vogue Dolls**, Izen/Stover	$29.95
5904	Collector's Guide to **Celebrity Dolls**, Spurgeon	$24.95
5599	Collector's Guide to **Dolls of the 1960s and 1970s**, Sabulis	$24.95
6030	Collector's Guide to **Horsman Dolls**, Jensen	$29.95
6025	**Doll Values**, Antique to Modern, 6th Ed., Moyer	$12.95
6032	**Madame Alexander** Collector's Dolls Price Guide #27, Crowsey	$12.95
6033	**Modern Collectible Dolls**, Volume VI, Moyer	$24.95
5689	**Nippon Dolls** & Playthings, Van Patten/Lau	$29.95
5365	**Peanuts Collectibles**, Podley/Bang	$24.95
6026	**Small Dolls of the 40s & 50s**, Stover	$29.95
5253	Story of **Barbie**, 2nd Ed., Westenhouser	$24.95
5277	**Talking Toys** of the 20th Century, Lewis	$15.95
2084	**Teddy Bears, Annalee's & Steiff** Animals, 3rd Series, Mandel	$19.95
5371	**Teddy Bear** Treasury, Yenke	$19.95
1808	Wonder of **Barbie**, Manos	$9.95
1430	World of **Barbie** Dolls, Manos	$9.95
4880	World of **Raggedy Ann** Collectibles, Avery	$24.95

TOYS & MARBLES

2333	Antique & Collectible **Marbles**, 3rd Ed., Grist	$9.95
4559	Collectible **Action Figures**, 2nd Ed., Manos	$17.95
2338	Collector's Encyclopedia of **Disneyana**, Longest, Stern	$24.95
5900	Collector's Guide to **Battery Toys**, 2nd Edition, Hultzman	$24.95
4566	Collector's Guide to **Tootsietoys**, 2nd Ed., Richter	$19.95
5169	Collector's Guide to **TV Toys** & Memorabilia, 2nd Ed., Davis/Morgan	$24.95
5360	**Fisher-Price Toys**, Cassity	$19.95
5593	Grist's Big Book of **Marbles**, 2nd Ed.	$24.95
3970	Grist's Machine-Made & Contemporary **Marbles**, 2nd Ed.	$9.95
5267	**Matchbox Toys**, 1947 to 1998, 3rd Ed., Johnson	$19.95
5830	**McDonald's** Collectibles, 2nd Edition, Henriques/DuVall	$24.95
5673	Modern **Candy Containers** & Novelties, Brush/Miller	$19.95
1540	Modern **Toys** 1930–1980, Baker	$19.95
5920	**Schroeder's Collectible Toys**, Antique to Modern Price Guide, 8th Ed.	$17.95
5908	**Toy Car** Collector's Guide, Johnson	$19.95

FURNITURE

3716	American **Oak** Furniture, Book II, McNerney	$12.95
1118	Antique **Oak** Furniture, Hill	$7.95
3720	Collector's Encyclopedia of **American** Furniture, Vol. III, Swedberg	$24.95
5359	Early **American** Furniture, Obbard	$12.95
1755	Furniture of the **Depression Era**, Swedberg	$19.95
3906	**Heywood-Wakefield** Modern Furniture, Rouland	$18.95
1885	**Victorian** Furniture, Our American Heritage, McNerney	$9.95
3829	**Victorian** Furniture, Our American Heritage, Book II, McNerney	$9.95

JEWELRY, HATPINS, WATCHES & PURSES

4704	Antique & Collectible **Buttons**, Wisniewski	$19.95
1748	Antique **Purses**, Revised Second Ed., Holiner	$19.95
4850	Collectible **Costume Jewelry**, Simonds	$24.95
5675	Collectible **Silver Jewelry**, Rezazadeh	$24.95
3722	Collector's Ency. of **Compacts**, Carryalls & Face Powder Boxes, Mueller	$24.95
4940	**Costume Jewelry**, A Practical Handbook & Value Guide, Rezazadeh	$24.95
5812	Fifty Years of Collectible **Fashion Jewelry**, 1925–1975, Baker	$24.95
1424	**Hatpins** & Hatpin Holders, Baker	$9.95
5695	**Ladies' Vintage Accessories**, Bruton	$24.95
1181	100 Years of Collectible **Jewelry**, 1850–1950, Baker	$9.95
4729	**Sewing Tools** & Trinkets, Thompson	$24.95
6038	**Sewing Tools** & Trinkets, Volume 2, Thompson	$24.95
6039	Signed Beauties of **Costume Jewelry**, Brown	$24.95
5620	Unsigned Beauties of **Costume Jewelry**, Brown	$24.95
4878	Vintage & Contemporary **Purse Accessories**, Gerson	$24.95
5696	Vintage & Vogue Ladies' **Compacts**, 2nd Edition, Gerson	$29.95
5923	**Vintage Jewelry** for Investment & Casual Wear, Edeen	$24.95

INDIANS, GUNS, KNIVES, TOOLS, PRIMITIVES

1868	Antique **Tools**, Our American Heritage, McNerney	$9.95
5616	Big Book of **Pocket Knives**, Stewart	$19.95
4943	Field Guide to Flint **Arrowheads & Knives** of the North American Indian	$9.95
2279	**Indian Artifacts** of the Midwest, Book I, Hothem	$14.95
3885	**Indian Artifacts** of the Midwest, Book II, Hothem	$16.95
4870	**Indian Artifacts** of the Midwest, Book III, Hothem	$18.95
5685	**Indian Artifacts** of the Midwest, Book IV, Hothem	$19.95
6132	**Modern Guns**, Identification & Values, 14th Ed., Quertermous	$14.95
2164	**Primitives**, Our American Heritage, McNerney	$9.95
1759	**Primitives**, Our American Heritage, 2nd Series, McNerney	$14.95
6031	Standard **Knife** Collector's Guide, 4th Ed., Ritchie & Stewart	$14.95
5999	**Wilderness** Survivor's Guide, Hamper	$12.95

PAPER COLLECTIBLES & BOOKS

4633	**Big Little Books**, Jacobs	$18.95
5902	**Boys' & Girls' Book** Series	$19.95
4710	Collector's Guide to **Children's Books**, 1850 to 1950, Volume I, Jones	$18.95
5153	Collector's Guide to **Children's Books**, 1850 to 1950, Volume II, Jones	$19.95
5596	Collector's Guide to **Children's Books**, 1950 to 1975, Volume III, Jones	$19.95
1441	Collector's Guide to **Post Cards**, Wood	$9.95
2081	Guide to Collecting **Cookbooks**, Allen	$14.95
5825	Huxford's **Old Book** Value Guide, 13th Ed.	$19.95
2080	Price Guide to **Cookbooks & Recipe Leaflets**, Dickinson	$9.95
3973	**Sheet Music** Reference & Price Guide, 2nd Ed., Pafik & Guiheen	$19.95
6041	Vintage **Postcards for the Holidays**, Reed	$24.95
4733	**Whitman Juvenile Books**, Brown	$17.95

GLASSWARE

5602	Anchor Hocking's **Fire-King** & More, 2nd Ed.	$24.95
4561	Collectible **Drinking Glasses**, Chase & Kelly	$17.95
5823	Collectible **Glass Shoes**, 2nd Edition, Wheatley	$24.95
5897	Coll. **Glassware from the 40s, 50s & 60s**, 6th Ed., Florence	$19.95
1810	Collector's Encyclopedia of **American Art Glass**, Shuman	$29.95
5907	Collector's Encyclopedia of **Depression Glass**, 15th Ed., Florence	$19.95
1961	Collector's Encyclopedia of **Fry Glassware**, Fry Glass Society	$24.95
1664	Collector's Encyclopedia of **Heisey Glass**, 1925–1938, Bredehoft	$24.95
3905	Collector's Encyclopedia of **Milk Glass**, Newbound	$24.95
4936	Collector's Guide to **Candy Containers**, Dezso/Poirier	$19.95
5820	Collector's Guide to **Glass Banks**, Reynolds	$24.95
4564	**Crackle Glass**, Weitman	$19.95
4941	**Crackle Glass**, Book II, Weitman	$19.95
4714	**Czechoslovakian Glass** and Collectibles, Book II, Barta/Rose	$16.95
5528	Early American **Pattern Glass**, Metz	$17.95
6125	**Elegant Glassware** of the Depression Era, 10th Ed., Florence	$24.95
3981	Evers' Standard **Cut Glass** Value Guide	$12.95
5614	Field Guide to **Pattern Glass**, McCain	$17.95
5615	Florence's **Glassware Pattern Identification** Guide, Vol. II	$19.95
4719	**Fostoria**, Etched, Carved & Cut Designs, Vol. II, Kerr	$24.95
3883	**Fostoria Stemware**, The Crystal for America, Long/Seate	$24.95

5261	**Fostoria Tableware**, 1924 – 1943, Long/Seate	$24.95
5361	**Fostoria Tableware**, 1944 – 1986, Long/Seate	$24.95
5604	**Fostoria**, Useful & Ornamental, Long/Seate	$29.95
5899	**Glass & Ceramic Baskets**, White	$19.95
4644	**Imperial Carnival Glass**, Burns	$18.95
5827	**Kitchen Glassware** of the Depression Years, 6th Ed., Florence	$24.95
5600	Much More Early American **Pattern Glass**, Metz	$17.95
5915	**Northwood Carnival Glass**, 1908 – 1925, Burns	$19.95
6136	Pocket Guide to **Depression Glass**, 13th Ed., Florence	$12.95
6023	Standard Encyclopedia of **Carnival Glass**, 8th Ed., Edwards/Carwile	$29.95
6024	Standard **Carnival Glass** Price Guide, 13th Ed., Edwards/Carwile	$9.95
6035	Standard Encyclopedia of **Opalescent Glass**, 4th Ed., Edwards/Carwile	$24.95
4732	**Very Rare Glassware** of the Depression Years, 5th Series, Florence	$24.95
4656	**Westmoreland Glass**, Wilson	$24.95

POTTERY

4927	**ABC Plates & Mugs**, Lindsay	$24.95
4929	**American Art Pottery**, Sigafoose	$24.95
4630	**American Limoges**, Limoges	$24.95
1312	**Blue & White Stoneware**, McNerney	$9.95
1959	**Blue Willow**, 2nd Ed., Gaston	$14.95
4851	Collectible **Cups & Saucers**, Harran	$18.95
5901	Collecting **Blue Willow**, Harman	$19.95
1373	Collector's Encyclopedia of **American Dinnerware**, Cunningham	$24.95
4931	Collector's Encyclopedia of **Bauer Pottery**, Chipman	$24.95
4658	Collector's Encyclopedia of **Brush-McCoy Pottery**, Huxford	$24.95
5034	Collector's Encyclopedia of **California Pottery**, 2nd Ed., Chipman	$24.95
3723	Collector's Encyclopedia of **Cookie Jars**, Book II, Roerig	$24.95
4939	Collector's Encyclopedia of **Cookie Jars**, Book III, Roerig	$24.95
5748	Collector's Encyclopedia of **Fiesta**, 9th Ed., Huxford	$24.95
3961	Collector's Encyclopedia of **Early Noritake**, Alden	$24.95
3812	Collector's Encyclopedia of **Flow Blue China**, 2nd Ed., Gaston	$24.95
3431	Collector's Encyclopedia of **Homer Laughlin China**, Jasper	$24.95
1276	Collector's Encyclopedia of **Hull Pottery**, Roberts	$19.95
3962	Collector's Encyclopedia of **Lefton China**, DeLozier	$19.95
4855	Collector's Encyclopedia of **Lefton China**, Book II, DeLozier	$19.95
5609	Collector's Encyclopedia of **Limoges Porcelain**, 3rd Ed., Gaston	$29.95
2334	Collector's Encyclopedia of **Majolica Pottery**, Katz-Marks	$19.95
1358	Collector's Encyclopedia of **McCoy Pottery**, Huxford	$19.95
5677	Collector's Encyclopedia of **Niloak**, 2nd Edition, Gifford	$29.95
3837	Collector's Encyclopedia of **Nippon Porcelain**, Van Patten	$24.95
1665	Collector's Ency. of **Nippon Porcelain**, 3rd Series, Van Patten	$24.95
5053	Collector's Ency. of **Nippon Porcelain**, 5th Series, Van Patten	$24.95
5678	Collector's Ency. of **Nippon Porcelain**, 6th Series, Van Patten	$29.95
1447	Collector's Encyclopedia of **Noritake**, Van Patten	$19.95
4951	Collector's Encyclopedia of **Old Ivory China**, Hillman	$24.95
5564	Collector's Encyclopedia of **Pickard China**, Reed	$29.95
3877	Collector's Encyclopedia of **R.S. Prussia**, 4th Series, Gaston	$24.95
5679	Collector's Encyclopedia of **Red Wing Art Pottery**, Dollen	$24.95
5618	Collector's Encyclopedia of **Rosemeade Pottery**, Dommel	$24.95
5841	Collector's Encyclopedia of **Roseville Pottery**, Revised, Huxford/Nickel	$24.95
5842	Collector's Encyclopedia of **Roseville Pottery**, 2nd Series, Huxford/Nickel	$24.95
5917	Collector's Encyclopedia of **Russel Wright**, 3rd Editon, Kerr	$29.95
4713	Collector's Encyclopedia of **Salt Glaze Stoneware**, Taylor/Lowrance	$24.95
5370	Collector's Encyclopedia of **Stangl Dinnerware**, Runge	$24.95
5921	Collector's Encyclopedia of **Stangl Artware**, Lamps, and Birds, RUnge	$29.95
3314	Collector's Encyclopedia of **Van Briggle Art Pottery**, Sasicki	$24.95
4563	Collector's Encyclopedia of **Wall Pockets**, Newbound	$19.95
2111	Collector's Encyclopedia of **Weller Pottery**, Huxford	$29.95
5680	Collector's Guide to **Feather Edge Ware**, McAllister	$19.95
3876	Collector's Guide to **Lu-Ray Pastels**, Meehan	$18.95
3814	Collector's Guide to **Made in Japan Ceramics**, White	$18.95
4646	Collector's Guide to **Made in Japan Ceramics**, Book II, White	$18.95
2339	Collector's Guide to **Shawnee Pottery**, Vanderbilt	$19.95
1425	**Cookie Jars**, Westfall	$9.95
3440	**Cookie Jars**, Book II, Westfall	$19.95

5909	**Dresden Porcelain** Studios, Harran	$29.95
5918	Florence's Big Book of **Salt & Pepper Shakers**	$24.95
2379	Lehner's Ency. of **U.S. Marks** on Pottery, Porcelain & China	$24.95
4722	**McCoy Pottery**, Collector's Reference & Value Guide, Hanson/Nissen	$19.95
5913	**McCoy Pottery**, Volume III, Hanson & Nissen	$24.95
5691	**Post86 Fiesta**, Identification & Value Guide, Racheter	$19.95
1670	**Red Wing Collectibles**, DePasquale	$9.95
1440	**Red Wing Stoneware**, DePasquale	$9.95
6037	**Rookwood Pottery**, Nicholson & Thomas	$24.95
1632	**Salt & Pepper Shakers**, Guarnaccia	$9.95
5091	**Salt & Pepper Shakers** II, Guarnaccia	$18.95
3443	**Salt & Pepper Shakers** IV, Guarnaccia	$18.95
3738	**Shawnee Pottery**, Mangus	$24.95
4629	Turn of the Century **American Dinnerware**, 1880s–1920s, Jasper	$24.95
3327	**Watt Pottery** – Identification & Value Guide, Morris	$19.95
5924	**Zanesville Stoneware** Company, Rans, Ralston & Russell	$24.95

OTHER COLLECTIBLES

5916	Advertising **Paperweights**, Holiner & Kammerman	$24.95
5838	Advertising **Thermometers**, Merritt	$16.95
5898	Antique & Contemporary **Advertising Memorabilia**, Summers	$24.95
5814	Antique **Brass & Copper** Collectibles, Gaston	$24.95
1880	Antique **Iron**, McNerney	$9.95
3872	Antique **Tins**, Dodge	$24.95
4845	Antique **Typewriters & Office Collectibles**, Rehr	$19.95
5607	Antiquing and Collecting on the **Internet**, Parry	$12.95
1128	**Bottle** Pricing Guide, 3rd Ed., Cleveland	$7.95
3718	Collectible **Aluminum**, Grist	$16.95
4560	Collectible **Cats**, An Identification & Value Guide, Book II, Fyke	$19.95
5060	Collectible **Souvenir Spoons**, Bednersh	$19.95
5676	Collectible **Souvenir Spoons**, Book II, Bednersh	$29.95
5666	Collector's Encyclopedia of **Granite Ware**, Book 2, Greguire	$29.95
5836	Collector's Guide to **Antique Radios**, 5th Ed., Bunis	$19.95
3966	Collector's Guide to **Inkwells**, Identification & Values, Badders	$18.95
4947	Collector's Guide to **Inkwells**, Book II, Badders	$19.95
5681	Collector's Guide to **Lunchboxes**, White	$19.95
5621	Collector's Guide to **Online Auctions**, Hix	$12.95
4652	Collector's Guide to **Transistor Radios**, 2nd Ed., Bunis	$16.95
4864	Collector's Guide to **Wallace Nutting Pictures**, Ivankovich	$18.95
1629	**Doorstops**, Identification & Values, Bertoia	$9.95
5683	**Fishing Lure** Collectibles, 2nd Ed., Murphy/Edmisten	$29.95
5911	**Flea Market Trader**, 13th Ed., Huxford	$9.95
4945	**G-Men and FBI Toys** and Collectibles, Whitworth	$18.95
6029	**Garage Sale & Flea Market Annual**, 10th Ed.	$19.95
3819	**General Store** Collectibles, Wilson	$24.95
5912	The **Heddon** Legacy, A Century of Classic **Lures**, Roberts & Pavey	$29.95
2216	**Kitchen Antiques**, 1790–1940, McNerney	$14.95
5991	**Lighting Devices** & Accessories of the 17th – 19th Centuries, Hamper	$9.95
5686	**Lighting Fixtures** of the Depression Era, Book I, Thomas	$24.95
4950	The **Lone Ranger**, Collector's Reference & Value Guide, Felbinger	$18.95
6028	Modern **Fishing Lure** Collectibles, Lewis	$24.95
2026	**Railroad** Collectibles, 4th Ed., Baker	$14.95
5619	**Roy Rogers and Dale Evans** Toys & Memorabilia, Coyle	$24.95
5919	**Schroeder's Antiques Price Guide**, 20th Ed., Huxford	$14.95
5007	**Silverplated Flatware**, Revised 4th Edition, Hagan	$18.95
6040	**Star Wars** Super Collector's Wish Book, Carlton	$29.95
6139	Summers' Guide to **Coca-Cola**, 4th Ed.	$24.95
5905	Summers' Pocket Guide to **Coca-Cola**, 3rd Ed.	$12.95
3892	**Toy & Miniature Sewing Machines**, Thomas	$18.95
4876	**Toy & Miniature Sewing Machines**, Book II, Thomas	$24.95
3977	Value Guide to **Gas Station Memorabilia**, Summers & Priddy	$24.95
4877	Vintage **Bar Ware**, Visakay	$24.95
5925	The Vintage Era of **Golf Club Collectibles**, John	$29.95
6010	The Vintage Era of **Golf Club Collectibles** Collector's Log, John	$9.95
6036	Vintage **Quilts**, Aug, Newman & Roy	$24.95
4935	The W.F. Cody **Buffalo Bill** Collector's Guide with Values	$24.95

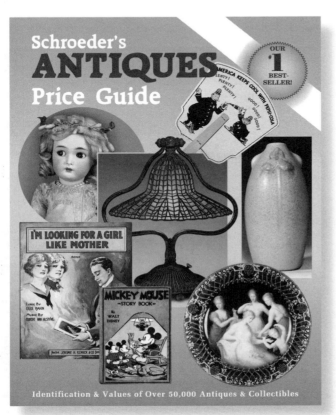